To Kayla Belle,

I can't wait to play golf with you.

Careers in Golf

An Insider's Guide to
Careers in the Golf Industry

Nancy Berkley

NATIONAL GOLF FOUNDATION ®

International Standard Book Number: 1-57701-091-4
National Golf Foundation Item Number: 99GEB01

Published by: National Golf Foundation,
                  1150 S. U.S. Highway 1, Suite 401
                  Jupiter, Florida, 33477
                  www.ngf.org

Manufactured in the United States of America

CONTENTS

ACKNOWLEDGEMENTS

My thanks to two Richards:

Two authors have inspired this book on a very personal level. The first is a popular children's writer, Richard Scary. His book *What Do People Do All Day?* has been read by and to millions of children. His illustrations of "Busytown," with many different people doing many different things, made a lasting impression on me. I am always illustrating the golf industry in my mind's eye à la Richard Scary.

Imagine a Richard Scary golf course in Busytown. There's a mechanic fixing a mower, a salesman delivering parts for the machine, and a superintendent looking over a green. Off on the side, golfers dressed in classic golf attire are riding down the fairway in a cart with bulging golf bags toward a clubhouse in the distance with a waiter serving drinks on the patio, the club manager working in his office, and the pro shop staff greeting golfers. So many busy people in so many careers in the golf industry!

I also have been inspired by Richard Nelson Bolles, author of *What Color is Your Parachute?* published by Ten Speed Press, Berkeley, Calif. – a top career book published annually and boasting six million copies in print. I encourage every reader of this book to read Dick's book as well. He has inspired me and I thank him.

Special thanks to my friends at the National Golf Foundation who have been both supportive and patient. I could not have completed this book without the help of Tara Gravel, senior editor at *GOLF Magazine*. Thank you, Tara, *especially for your substantive input.*

And a loving and sincere thank you to my husband, Peter, and my children, Jim, John, Alison and David for their help and encouragement.

I also want to acknowledge the efforts of the hundreds of members of the industry who responded to research surveys and answered my telephone calls. And in particular, to the following people who were especially helpful: Tad Altman, Mike Anderson, Brett Avery, John Baker, Jim Barrett, Jan Beljan, Ruffin Beckwith, Kathy Bissell, Desane Blaney, Jane Broderick, Doug Buffington, Jamie Carbone, Tammy Carvajal, Betsy Clark, Rob Cowen, Jack Dillon, Bob Dodds, Maria Erickson, Anne-Marie Fanguy, Dan Friedman, Kim Heck, Lee Hetrick, JoAnn Hoffman, Chris Hunkler, Barry Hyde, Allan Irwin, Pat Jones, Marty Kavanaugh, Chip King, K.C. Kinsey, Brad Klein, Mike Klemme, Bill Kubly, Ran Lavoie, Rebecca Luczycki, Mike Matthews, Ann Marquardt, Rich Mazzella, Michael McCarthy, Chris McKay, Melissa Montague,

Karen Moraghan, Jay Mottola, Tom Moynihan, Kara Norman, Kevin O'Connor, Diane Ogle, Larry Olmsted, M.G. Orender, Barry Palm, Tom Perry, John Piersol, Robert Pedrero, Greg Raleigh, Gary Rosmarin, Dick Rugge, Michael Schlesinger, Bill Seline, Greg Smith, Norm Spitzig, John Steinmann, Stina Sternberg, Larry Sugarman, Dave Tourville, Bobby Weed, John Wildmon, Lloyd Williams and Roger Yaffe.

A few words from the author:

When the National Golf Foundation, a leader in providing business information to the golf industry, asked me to consider writing a book about careers in the golf industry, I was immediately enthusiastic. Although I have been a golfer – just a good bogey golfer – for many years, I am a relative newcomer in my present career as a golf writer. As a newcomer to the golf industry, I know how overwhelming and complex this industry is.

But the more I thought about accepting the NGF's offer, the more it seemed that maybe I was just the right person to tackle this subject. Over the years, I had become a "career expert."

First was my sales career – a part-time job during high school and college. Then came my career as a high school English teacher. Next came my child-raising career. Then came law school and several years as an associate in a large law firm. Finally, after attending business school, I moved into marketing and strategic planning at a large financial services company. It's a wonder I had time to play golf at all during all those careers, but I did. And because I did, and because I truly enjoy the game, I landed in my current profession as a golf writer.

This book finally allows me to weave my broad and varied experiences together and offer some clarity and insight into choosing a career in the golf industry. I firmly believe that working in this industry should not just be a matter of luck. The industry is increasingly "professional" and a career in it should be something that you can prepare for and plan on.

The goal of this book is to help you select the career that suits your interests and skills. My mission is to help you find *your* career in the golf industry.

Nancy Berkley

CHAPTER ONE

Do You Speak "Golf?"

"If you're puzzled as to what field you'd like to be in for your next career or job, begin by asking yourself what language or languages you love to listen to, speak, and work in all day long. As a general rule, if you enjoy the language you deal with all day, then you will be happy in that field or career."

> Richard Nelson Bolles, Author,
> *What Color is Your Parachute?*
> (Ten Speed Press, Berkeley, Calif., 1998)

This book is for people looking for a career in the golf industry. It is for people who:

- like golf; or
- think they would like golf; or,
- want to work with or around people who like golf.

It is for people who may not know what they want to do, but think they know where they want to do it. *This book is for people who speak "golf."*

You do not have to be a good golfer to read this book or to find a career in the golf industry. And, although a college degree is helpful, many positions in the industry are open to high school graduates with strong personal skills and work ethics.

It may not be easy to find that perfect job. But it is well worth the effort because people working in the golf industry generally love what they do.

Why should you read this book?

Whether you are just beginning to think about possible careers or are now thinking about making a career change, this book will help you. After taking our guided tour through the industry's many sectors and businesses, you will be in a better position to find your opportunity within it.

You may need some help because the golf industry is very large and fragmented, which makes it difficult to identify where employment opportunities exist. (More about a "fragmented" industry a little later.)

"Help Wanted" sections of newspapers seldom have "golf" sections. This means people looking for positions must check the classified sections of golf publications to find employment opportunities. Although

Internet job sites are extremely helpful – including the new golf-specific employment sites – they often assume you know how the industry is organized.

This book provides the background you need for your job search. You will read about careers that are familiar and about some that you never knew existed. You will find an opportunity that fits your skills, ambitions and interests.

This book also will help you become a better-educated job candidate. In understanding the industry, you will be able to ask the right questions and offer good answers in an interview. Your chances of landing that perfect job will improve.

And finally, you should read this book because there is no other book like it to help you navigate the industry.

Do you have to be a good golfer to work in the golf industry?

Many people worry that they need to be a scratch golfer or low handicapper to work in the industry. The truth is that you do not always have to be a good golfer. Except in a few positions, such as *golf instructor* or *director of golf operations*, your interest and appreciation of the game is more important than your skill as a golfer.

As you will discover, the golf industry has careers for people of different skills and educational backgrounds. Some careers require a college degree, while others stress on-the-job training and work experience. Some positions require managerial skills, while others require sales, administrative or even technical and mechanical aptitude.

What if you need to be a better golfer?

Let's say that after reading the section on *independent sales reps* in Chapter 6, you are convinced that a career in sales is right for you. You've read that sales reps for golf equipment manufacturers often spend time playing golf with potential customers. That makes you nervous. You play golf, but are you good enough?

Maybe you are and maybe you're not. The good news is that with good instruction and practice you will be able to improve your game.

To learn more about where to find golf instruction in your area, visit your local golf courses and talk to the head professional or golf instructor. Or consider attending a golf school. And then – practice, practice, practice.

To apply for jobs you will have to know how to describe your golf ability. If you don't have an official handicap, you should be able to describe your playing experience or perhaps even your potential.

And as part of your learning experience, make sure you play with seasoned and experienced golfers. An on-course playing lesson with a golf pro is an excellent investment in your career, because you will learn the terminology, etiquette and culture of the game. Knowing these things is more important than your handicap or how far you hit your driver.

How will you know which career is right for you?

In deciding which career is right for you, you should analyze your skills and interests. Let's continue with our sales-career example: After reading about the independent sales representative, you may have concluded that you do not have the required discipline and self-motivation. Your next step is to look for other types of sales positions that have more structure, such as company reps.

If you have good mechanical and technical abilities, you may be interested in positions in equipment design or maintenance – or even golf club repair. Or you may be excited to learn that there are several computer specialties within the industry.

You will be in charge of your career decisions, but this book will educate you about your options.

You do not have to take this tour of the industry alone. If you are in high school or college, consider speaking with your guidance or career counselor. He or she should have many tests and tools to help you match your skills and interests with specific careers.

If you are already in the job market and considering a change, you probably already know where your skills lay. If you are not sure, consider seeing a professional career counselor.

Why is job networking important?

The saying, "It's not what you know, but who you know," holds true in the golf industry. Although many positions, especially with large manufacturers, are advertised, lots of openings are filled by word-of-mouth. The ability to make friends who become part of your career "network" is important.

If you play regularly at a golf course, get to know the staff. If you are in a college program, stay in touch with your classmates. If you are already working in the industry, get to know your colleagues. One of the best networking opportunities is to join a golf association and participate in its events. It's good to establish a broad network of contacts.

Are internships available in the industry?

An internship is a supervised work experience usually offered to students who are looking for practical work experience in their chosen profession. Internships can be paid or unpaid.

One of the most well-known internship programs is the USGA's P.J. Boatwright, Jr. Internships, which place students at golf associations across the country. (The USGA also offers fellowships and grants.) See the "Foundation" section of www.usga.org.

Many of the state and regional golf associations (described in Chapter 2) also offer internships, although they may not be widely advertised. One regional association runs an excellent internship program for high school students. GOLFWORKS, sponsored by the Metropolitan Golf Association, which serves the greater New York City area, places inner-city students in jobs at area clubs. Go to their Web site at www.mgagolf.org for programs sponsored by the Metropolitan Golf Association.

Also of note are the internships offered by the National Minority Golf Foundation, established in 1995 to increase minority participation in the game and industry. See www.nmgf.org.

Some of the golf employment Web sites described later in this chapter allow you to search for internships, or you can use your initiative to contact the associations and businesses listed in this book. Your call may encourage them to set up internship programs if none exist.

How is this book organized?

The book is organized as a guided tour of the industry, with each chapter visiting a different industry segment. After an introduction to some of the key organizations that influence the industry, the tour shifts to facility development and moves on through facility management, manufacturing, retail operations, instruction, and event management. We conclude with careers in marketing, public relations and the media.

The careers and chapters are organized using the same categories that the publisher, the National Golf Foundation, uses to gather industry statistics. (The National Golf Foundation has more than 6,000 members from all industry segments and is a leading source of industry research and information.)

The first half of each chapter provides an overview of one golf industry sector and introduces careers, occupations and professions within that sector. Occupations and professions are in **bold**, ***italic type*** the first time they appear in a chapter.

The second half of the chapter, titled "Careers to Explore," includes descriptions of careers – with major careers detailed in "Career Close-ups." More than 55 careers are covered. Each chapter also features an interview with a successful industry leader, along with practical "Job Hunting Tips."

To help readers find an entrance into the industry, each chapter also includes the names and Web sites of related businesses or associations. The Appendix also lists detailed contact information.

How were careers selected for the book?

In order to be included, an occupation had to meet the following criteria:

1. First, there had to be a *significant number of openings or opportunities*. Careers with just a handful of positions – such as the club repairers who travel with the professional tours – were not included.

2. Next, the careers had to be *those for which you could prepare*, that is, through courses or particular work experience.

3. The third criterion was that the career had to be in a *stable or expanding sector of the industry*.

4. The fourth criterion was that the career required *an interest in, knowledge of, or playing expertise in golf*. If you wonder why scuba divers who retrieve balls from water hazards are not included, it is because they can know nothing about the game and still be excellent at what they do.

5. Finally, we selected careers that would appeal *to readers with many different skills*. Some careers require an understanding of mechanics. Others require scientific knowledge about agriculture or turf management. Many more require managerial or administrative skills – or expertise in sales and marketing.

What is included in each job description?

In the "Careers to Explore" sections, information is organized whenever possible around the following topics: Duties, Salary Range, Entry-level Positions, Golf Ability & Interest, Special Skills & Personal Traits, and Career Ladder & Promotion Prospects.

How was information gathered?

In the preparation for this book, I developed a three-page survey asking people in many different occupations 15 questions about their jobs. The National Golf Foundation sent the survey to several hundred of its members in various industry sectors.

I reviewed the responses and followed up with personal interviews. With the information I gathered, I was able to create career descriptions based on the experience of real people.

The process enabled me to learn much about each segment of the industry – and how they relate to one another.

What is the source of salary information?

Salary information is based on the surveys mentioned above. When possible, I checked the information against other sources. For certain occupations, information came from annual salary surveys conducted by the National Golf Foundation. (Information based on NGF research is noted as such.) One word of caution: While I believe the salary ranges listed were accurate at the time of publication, salaries can vary significantly based on a number of factors, including geographic region.

How should you use this book?

If it is early in your career-planning process and you know only that you would like to work in the golf industry, I suggest you read this book cover to cover.

If you know that you want to work in a particular profession, such as sales, use the index to find that position. Positions with the same title may be described in different chapters. For example, manufacturer's sales reps are in Chapter 6 – Careers With Manufacturers, while sales positions in golf shops are in Chapter 7 – Careers in Retail.

You will notice that there is a wide margin on each page. It's intended for your personal notes. It's a good place to write items you discover on a Web site, or the names of people you have contacted.

Where are some other sources of career information?

I wish I could say that all you have to do to find your career in the golf industry is to read this book. Unfortunately, that is not the case.

You may find general career books helpful. My favorite is *What Color Is Your Parachute?* by Richard Nelson Bolles (Ten Speed Press, Berkeley, Calif.), which is published annually. It includes advice and references on job-hunting skills such as résumé writing and interviews.

As your search advances, you may want to contact companies directly. Industry directories or guides that list names and addresses of businesses and associations are helpful – especially when organized by profession. The NGF publishes several directories; check www.ngf.org. Some professional organizations and associations (listed throughout the book) also publish directories or list members on their Web sites.

No discussion of career resources is complete without a mention of executive recruiters. Executive recruiters are hired by companies to find qualified applicants. The company pays the recruiters' fees – often up to one-third of the employee's annual salary. Recruiters generally have their own contacts and don't rely on résumés received in the mail. But if you are considering a lateral move from another industry, it may be worthwhile to contact a recruiter specializing in golf. *The Directory of Executive Recruiters 2001* (Kennedy Publications, Fitzwilliam, N.H.) can help you find one.

How can the Internet help your search?

I couldn't imagine writing this book without the help of the Internet. It has been an invaluable research tool and it will be for you too.

Here are my suggestions for using the Internet:

Become familiar with the employment Web sites devoted to the golf industry.

➤ One of the easiest to use is www.golfsurfin.com. This site is free to job-seekers (employers pay to list positions). You can search by profession or by employers.

➤ www.usgolfjobs.com is another good site. It is free to employers but charges job-seekers a monthly subscription. The search categories here are extensive.

➤ If you are looking for a job in the turf industry, use www.turfnet.com. This site is owned by Turnstile publications, which publishes *Golfweek*.

➤ www.golfingcareers.com, operated by one of the large employment Web-site developers, was launched in 2001.

➤ Many golf associations and companies include employment information on their Web sites.

Sometimes you have to be resourceful in using Web sites to find employment information. For example, Golfsmith is a well-known retailer with a good Web site, www.golfsmith.com. The site is designed for consumers, but the "About Us" section, which describes how the company was founded, includes a link to the "Employment" page. The page lists current openings and provides the name and address of the human resources director, who is the head of the personnel department.

If you want to broaden your search, look for employment Web sites in the general sports industry, such as www.jobsinsports.com or www.womensportsservices.com.

Note: Web sites are constantly under revision. I hope that those I recommend will continue to be helpful. It is a good idea to periodically use a general search engine (my favorite is www.google.com) using the words "golf," "careers" and "employment" to discover new sites. Also, when searching associations' sites, be careful about the use of .com and .org. Some organizations have .com sites.

Are there some skills that are important to all positions?

Yes! In doing research for this book, I can't tell you how many times employees listed computer, communication, management and leadership skills as essential to their jobs.

Computer proficiency is needed in many golf careers. Golf course superintendents use computers to manage pump and irrigation systems;

merchandise buyers use computer spread sheets for financial planning and reporting; project managers use management software; golf courses use computers to manage tee times; and designers use Global Positioning Systems and Computer Assisted Design technologies extensively.

Learning to communicate, manage and lead effectively may be more difficult than obtaining computer skills. Yet these skills are also critical in all career paths. Do whatever you can to develop them. If you are lucky enough to have good mentors, ask them to critique your ability in these areas.

GOLF INDUSTRY BASICS

How is the golf industry organized?

The golf industry is often referred to as a "cottage" or "fragmented" industry. In a fragmented industry there are many small, local manufacturers with informal distribution and communication. The opposite of a fragmented industry is a "concentrated" industry, such as the auto industry, where a few big players control most of the market.

Think of a visit to the shops in colonial Williamsburg where each cottage makes a different product. If you happened to live in Williamsburg in 1776 (at the time of the Declaration of Independence), you bought your candles at the cottage on Main Street where they were made. But if you lived in Philadelphia during that time, your candles came not from Williamsburg, but from your local cottage or home producer.

Although golf in the United States does not date back to colonial times, but to the late 19th century, its local cottage-like origins were similar. People played at local courses, built by local workers, and bought golf products from small local suppliers.

The golf industry then matured and become more concentrated as large firms with strong brand names came to dominate the manufacturing of clubs, balls and turf equipment. But many other sectors of the industry remain fragmented, with small and highly competitive businesses battling for market share.

Of course, when we read golf magazines, we notice the ads for the big companies. But most firms in the golf industry begin – and remain – as small local businesses with local customer bases.

How does a fragmented industry affect employment opportunities?

In a fragmented industry finding a job – or, the flip side, finding an employee – presents real challenges. Let's say I sent my résumé to two companies with powerful brand names, like Titleist or Wilson, simply because I knew their names and addresses. Unfortunately, I learned that they had no openings, or required more years of experience than I had. With thousands of courses and manufacturers across the country, where do I send my résumé now? I can't even find a golf category in the classified section of my newspaper.

The industry's fragmented nature means that finding a fulfilling job involves dedication, education and organization. That is why this book was written – to help you find your leads.

What are some important statistics about the golf industry?

The vitality of golf is reflected in the growth of the number of golfers over the past 50 years. The number of golfers was estimated in 1950 to be 3.5 million. In 2000, the number of golfers was estimated at 26.7 million. Growth has been influenced by televised events and highly visible professional and amateur golfers, and the game has become one of the most widely enjoyed leisure pastimes in the United States. Overall, the number of golfers has grown at a compound annual growth rate (CAGR) of 4.3 percent over the past 50 years.

Beginning in the early 1960s, the golf industry experienced a dramatic shift in the nature of golf course development. Prior to 1960, golf was primarily a private recreational activity restricted to America's elite society. As a result of the favorable economics of public courses as well as the ability to cater to a greater number of middle income players who were coming into the game, public golf began a significant growth period beginning in the 1960s.

Since 1986, golf has grown faster than motion pictures, financial services, hotels and communications, all of which generally are thought to be fast-growing industries. Only amusement and recreation in general have grown somewhat faster than golf in terms of revenues. Golf has been experiencing uniquely strong growth in both interest and in spending over the past decade and compares very favorably with other industries.

Overall growth in the industry in the past 15 years has come from a mix of favorable populations trends, increasing participation and increasing spending per golfer. This growth is estimated to be at a CAGR of 7.5 percent – as measured by spending on equipment, fees and apparel. When combined with the growth in golf course investment, nearly all sectors of the industry have benefited from strong growth in revenues.

The population is expected to increase in favorable golfing age groups as baby boomers and their children age. This growth is partially offset by Generation X, which is replacing baby boomers in the 30- to 49-year-old age bracket. As golfers age, they tend to play more frequently. Baby boomers alone will account for a 12 percent increase in the total size of the industry, which could have an impact of an additional 65 million rounds through 2010.

How do trends and cycles in the industry affect my opportunities?

In any given year, certain sectors in the industry will be up, while others are down. Golfers may be buying less equipment but spending more on greens fees – or just the opposite.

In spite of these economic cycles, American's passion for the game ensures that this will always be a solid industry in which to work. Awareness and trial are at an all-time high, and all the macro trends are favorable. In fact, a study undertaken by the National Golf Foundation in 1999 estimated that there were approximately 41 million people who said they would like to return to golf, learn the game or play more. That's a large untapped market in addition to the existing base of golfers.

Rather than worrying about industry ups and downs, I suggest you focus on finding a position in which you can excel – one that plays to your strengths. That is your best employment insurance.

What are the opportunities for women in the industry?

As a woman, I want to address this question. About 80 percent of all golfers are male, and it's likely that an even greater percentage of golf industry employees are male. When I walk the aisles of the big industry trade shows, I am especially aware of this.

But that does not mean women should not be encouraged to work in the industry – in fact, quite the contrary. The climate is especially favorable for women because there is much interest in growing the number of women golfers.

There are several occupations in which women seem to be gaining ground. According to the construction contractors and irrigation designers I interviewed, more women are being hired in construction management and course design.

The cover of the USGA's *Golf Journal* (November/December 2000), cited golf course designers Alice Dye, Jan Beljan, Sandy Bigler and Victoria Martz as prominent in the industry. I am sure you will enjoy our interview with Jan Beljan in Chapter 3.

Although it is still somewhat rare to see a woman driving heavy equipment on a construction site, there are more women working on maintenance crews on golf courses, especially in the Western states. And many superintendents reported that they would like to hire more women.

It is also well known in the industry that female golf professionals are in great demand, both as instructors and as facility managers.

Occasionally women may be challenged by stereotypes and generalizations, but if they can gain the experience needed for a profession, there are plenty of opportunities. To the women reading this book, and to the daughters and granddaughters of readers, I encourage you to find a home in golf.

CHAPTER TWO

Careers with Golf Associations

"Working for an association is one of the best jobs in the golf industry. It's an opportunity to help people work together for the betterment of the game."
Lee Hetrick, Executive Director
Golf Course Builders Association of America

In This Chapter:

- Why our career tour begins here
- What is an association?
- Who works at associations?
- Tips for discovering employment opportunities
- Learn about the following positions:
    Executive Director
    Project Director
    Marketing Director
    Publications Director
    Tournament Director
    Administrative Assistant
- An interview with Jay Mottola, Executive Director of the Metropolitan Golf Association

Why does our tour begin with associations?

When people think about working in golf, the first positions that come to mind are those of teaching pro or touring pro. Although it may surprise you, that is not where our tour of the industry begins. Follow along and you will understand why.

As explained in Chapter 1, the golf industry is fragmented, with thousands of businesses – mostly small to mid-size – producing thousands of products and services. In an industry with so many moving parts, something must set standards that hold all the pieces together and keep them moving in a positive direction.

Associations are the glue that holds the industry together. Becoming familiar with the different types of golf associations is a good introduction to the industry and a good place to begin identifying career opportunities.

What is an association?

In addition to the associations for recreational, amateur and professional golfers, there are associations that serve the professions within it.

Let's explore the definition and role of an association.

- An association, which also may be called an "organization" or "foundation" (the terms are used interchangeably in this chapter), is different from a traditional business. Most golf associations are not organized for profit. Sometimes they are described as "not-for-profits" or "non-profits." That is somewhat of a misnomer, because all associations try to raise enough revenue (through membership fees, grants or fundraising events) to cover expenses, including the salaries of employees.

- Associations serve members rather than customers. Instead of returning profits to shareholders or investors, not-for-profits take pride in providing services to their members or in supporting charitable endeavors.

- Associations don't manufacture or sell products – at least not in the traditional sense. Salaries may not be as high as in for-profit enterprises, but hours are often predictable and manageable and job satisfaction runs high. That may be the reason that people who start working in not-for-profits often spend their entire careers there.

- Golf associations are the key shapers of golf's future and offer challenging career opportunities.

Providing the foundation for the golf industry are the 21.4 million men and 5.2 million women who play the game in the U.S. (That's you and me!) The associations that serve our needs are organized *demographically* and *geographically*. For example, there are associations for junior, women, senior, and disabled golfers, and associations that serve geographic areas, such as state and regional golf associations. Of course, not every golfer belongs to an association, but the work of associations strengthens the game for everyone.

How do associations get started?

Associations usually are formed when people with common interests realize that their interests can be promoted more effectively when they act as a group. Following are some examples in the golf industry:

- The ***United States Golf Association*** (USGA), www.usga.org, was founded in 1894 by serious amateur golfers at several golf courses who were interested in establishing rules and standards for amateur competitions. Now more than 9,000 private and public golf courses are members of the USGA. And under the USGA Members Program, founded in 1975, 900,000 individual golfers have become

USGA members. More than ever it can be said that the USGA is run by golfers for *all* golfers, and, in the words of the USGA, "For the Good of the Game."

- *The Professional Golfers' Association of America* (The PGA of America), www.pga.com, is not only a highly recognized brand, but also a powerful association. Its approximately 27,000 members, including those in its apprentice program, are linked by their training as golf instructors and managers and by their commitment to a professional standard. The majority of golf facilities in this country employ at least one certified member of The PGA of America. In addition to its national headquarters in Palm Beach Gardens, Fla., the organization has state or regional sections all over the country.

- The *Golf Course Superintendents Association of America* (GCSAA), www.gcsaa.org, founded in 1926 by 60 greenkeepers, now has nearly 22,000 members. Through its efforts, the profession of golf course superintendent has grown in stature along with other occupations in the turf management sector.

Many organizations and associations were started to support professional or grass-roots causes. The National Golf Sales Representatives Association was founded by Tom Moynihan, an experienced sales representative who realized in 1987 that there was no network for sales representatives. With Tom's leadership, the NGSA grew to more than 3,000 members and provides a job clearinghouse for people interested in sales rep positions.

Two other associations that demonstrate the power of the individual are Rally for a Cure, founded by William Lawler, whose wife died of breast cancer, and the Susan G. Komen Breast Cancer Foundation, founded by Nancy Brinker, whose sister, Susan G. Komen, also died of breast cancer. Both have strong ties to women's golf, with millions of women sporting pink ribbons to show their support for breast cancer research.

Remember, however, that every large association started small. If you have an entrepreneurial spirit and recognize a need, you could start your own association. There are several good books that explain how, such as *Starting and Running a Nonprofit Organization* (University of Minnesota Press, 1996). If you do start your own association, you could even be its first executive director.

Who works at associations?

Associations are often headed by *executive directors*. (A few associations use the title *president*.) The executive director operates much like the chief executive officer or president of a for-profit business and reports to the association's board of directors or founders.

JOB HUNTING TIPS:

Attend an association's educational seminar

Many professional associations have certification and educational programs that can be helpful for job seekers from non-golf industries.

For example, if you have been working as a buyer in a large department store, you might find the seminars offered by the Association of Golf Merchandisers an excellent introduction to golf retailing.

In a large association, the executive director may have many *department directors* reporting to him or her. Following is a list of common positions in mid- to large-size associations: *membership director*, *media director*, *director of research*, *director of marketing*, *publications manager*, *tournament director*, *education director* and *project director*. If the association is large, there may also be *legal*, *financial and human resources directors*. Each director may have several *assistant directors*, and in turn, *administrative assistants*.

Keep in mind, however, that the executive director of a small association may wear the hats of many directors and have only one or two paid assistants. In the early days of an association, volunteers may be very important and, although unpaid, may deserve professional titles. Volunteering for a new association is a very good way to get experience.

What are the types of associations?

There are three different categories of associations: professional, demographic and geographic. You may prefer the work of one type of association rather than another.

- *Professional Associations* provide services to people in particular careers. Following are some professional associations. (See the Appendix for contact information and a brief explanation of all the associations referenced in this book).

  ➢ American Society of Golf Course Architects
  ➢ Association of Golf Merchandisers
  ➢ Club Managers Association of America
  ➢ Golf Course Builders Association of America
  ➢ Golf Course Superintendents Association of America
  ➢ Golf Manufacturers & Distributors Association
  ➢ Golf Range Association of America
  ➢ Golf Writers Association of America
  ➢ International Association of Golf Administrators
  ➢ International Network of Golf
  ➢ The National Association of Golf Tournament Directors
  ➢ National Club Association
  ➢ National Golf Course Owners Association
  ➢ National Golf Foundation
  ➢ National Golf Sales Representatives Association
  ➢ The PGA of America
  ➢ PGA TOUR
  ➢ PGA TOUR Tournaments Association

- *Demographic Associations* are organized according to the personal characteristics and interests of their members. Here are several examples:

  ➢ American Junior Golf Association

➤ Association of Disabled American Golfers

➤ Executive Women's Golf Association

➤ The First Tee

➤ National Minority Golf Foundation

➤ Senior Golfers Association of America

➤ World Golf Foundation

- *Geographic Associations* provide members with local services and information. Every state has either its own golf association or is part of a regional association. State and regional associations are closely aligned with the USGA, administering USGA handicaps to members and using USGA guidelines to set local course slopes and ratings. Many state and regional associations also have active tournament schedules.

    Following are three examples of geographic associations. Their Web sites show a breadth of activities and employment opportunities. Take a look at the Web site of your state golf association for opportunities closer to home.

    ➤ Greater Cincinnati Golf Association: www.gcga.org

    ➤ Metropolitan Golf Association, www.met.pga.com, serves the New York metropolitan area – including parts of New Jersey and Connecticut.

    ➤ Minnesota Golf Association: www.mngolf.org

> **JOB HUNTING TIPS:**
>
> **Visit www.usga.org for state links**
>
> A good way to learn about state and regional associations is to visit the "associations" section of www.usga.org, which has links to many state associations. Some state Web sites have employment pages. If not, call or write their listed addresses for more information.

CAREERS TO EXPLORE

Career Close-up: EXECUTIVE DIRECTOR

OVERVIEW: The *executive director* is the most senior position in associations. Openings don't occur frequently and the executive director is often promoted from a junior position within the association or a related one. Executive directors of large national associations have earned their senior status after years of successful management. As you read about this career, pay attention to the entry-level positions that can lead to the top.

DUTIES: The executive director has both leadership and management responsibilities. With the guidance of a board of directors or founding members, his or her major responsibility is to set the strategic direction and mission of the association. As a manager, the executive director also hires senior staff.

In large associations, motivating and managing a large number of employees is a very important part of the job. In addition, the executive director usually serves as the association's spokesperson; it is a highly visible position.

SALARY RANGE: The average annual salary of an executive director of a moderate-sized association is approximately $70,000. Executive directors of small associations earn closer to $40,000 annually. The holder of the top position at a large national association can earn more than $200,000 a year.

JOB OPPORTUNITIES: The number of golf associations is growing, which means that there are many job opportunities, especially if you are willing to start at a junior or administrative level. Senior directors do not frequently resign, or get fired or hired away; so, opportunities for advancement are somewhat limited. An exception may be in the marketing area, where associations must often reach outside of the golf industry for expertise.

EDUCATION & TRAINING: To reach the top spot in an association, a college degree is generally required, and a graduate degree, such as a master's in business administration (MBA), is a plus. Several graduate business schools now offer courses on management of not-for-profits. And degrees in business, marketing and communications are helpful.

Depending on an association's mission, a golf-specific education may be required. College degrees from Professional Golf Management programs (covered in Chapter 8) can be good preparation.

If an association is heavily involved in running tournaments – the case with many state and regional golf associations – knowledge of tournament management and the USGA Rules of Golf is essential.

Many trade associations are involved in collecting research on their industry sector. A statistical background may be helpful in those associations.

ENTRY-LEVEL POSITIONS: *Administrative assistant* is a key entry-level position. You may answer telephones and keep projects on schedule, but the position is an excellent opportunity to learn and will position you for promotion.

If you already have significant experience in a particular field, such as membership or marketing, look for more senior positions as *department director*.

Don't overlook volunteer positions, especially with state and regional golf associations. Not only will they provide valuable training, but the experience may prime you for a permanent position.

Volunteer opportunities are often available at association-sponsored tournaments. To learn more about volunteering at tournaments, contact your local state golf association or see Chapter 9 – Careers in Tour Management and Event Planning.

GOLF ABILITY & INTEREST: The executive director of a major golf association that promotes the game and sponsors tournaments should carry close to a single digit handicap. Executive directors of smaller trade and professional associations may not need low handicaps, but they must be comfortable playing golf with good players.

SPECIAL SKILLS & PERSONAL TRAITS: A good business background is helpful because, although an association does not sell services in the sense of for-profit businesses, its success depends on satisfied members.

CAREER LADDER & PROMOTION PROSPECTS: Promotion within an association is common, which is why it is worthwhile to take an entry-level position. As our research confirmed, the world of golf associations is tightly knit – everyone seems to know everyone else. If you earn a good reputation in one association, it may open opportunities for you in another.

> **SOUND BITES FROM EXECUTIVE DIRECTORS**
> **Positive**
> "Best job in the golf industry."
> **Negative**
> "Good and bad news travels fast."
> "The job can consume your personal life."

Career Close-up: PROJECT DIRECTOR

OVERVIEW: Running an association involves many administrative activities, such as maintaining membership records and preparing publications for members. But associations may also undertake projects that require special planning and management. For example, an organization may embark on a major membership or public relations campaign. Or it may plan an industry conference, undertake a research project or sponsor a tournament.

Projects are one-time happenings or events with clear objectives. Project management has become a trendy career in our fast-moving, results-oriented industry.

If a project is large, an association may hire a temporary or part-time *project director* or *project manager*. More frequently, however, a staff member will be asked to reallocate time to manage a special project. Accepting responsibility for a special project offers an excellent opportunity to show management ability.

DUTIES: Project managers must be able to see the "big picture," as well as all the component pieces. Planning and organization are major responsibilities. Projects are usually divided into distinct tasks. The manager assigns tasks to committees, teams or individuals, and sets a timetable. The challenge is to coordinate all the tasks so that the project is completed on time.

SALARY RANGE: $25,000 to $65,000 annually. Some project managers are paid on a project or hourly basis.

JOB OPPORTUNITIES & PROMOTION PROSPECTS: Associations are taking on increasingly more responsibilities and projects, so this is a field with ample opportunities. Once you develop project-managing skills, you may be offered positions as ***tournament director*** or ***event manager*** (see Chapter 9).

EDUCATION & TRAINING: A college education is preferred, but no specific major is required. You need to know whether you like managing complex projects or prefer being a "worker bee." If you don't like organizing and planning, this is not the career for you. Some very good software programs have been developed to help keep track of projects' component parts and timetables, so related computer experience is helpful.

ENTRY-LEVEL POSITIONS: Any administrative position that allows you to organize and execute a project – even a small one – is a good place to start. Do not reject clerical positions; once you are on the inside of an association, you are likely to find opportunities to demonstrate project management skills.

GOLF ABILITY & INTEREST: Because special projects are often separate from the regular services of an association, a project manager may not have to play golf as often or as well as senior executives. Most projects, however, require an understanding of the game and the industry. Planning tournaments requires extensive knowledge of tournament operations.

SPECIAL SKILLS & PERSONAL TRAITS: Project management depends on delegating responsibility. Timeliness is critical. If you are always running late, this is a career to avoid.

MARKETING DIRECTOR

The marketing positions in associations usually involve attracting and keeping members. Sometimes the position of ***marketing director*** is referred to as ***membership director***. The ability to understand and research the needs of members is a classic marketing exercise. The marketing director may also oversee public relations efforts, or there may be a separate ***director of public relations***. (Marketing careers are described more fully in Chapter 10.)

It sounds simple, but one of the key services associations provide is information about themselves. Almost all associations have newsletters, magazines or Web sites. An association may have a separate publications department and ***publications director***, or the position may fall within the marketing department. If you are interested in publications and media relations, there are appropriate positions in associations. (For information about careers in the media, see Chapter 11.)

TOURNAMENT DIRECTOR

Golf associations that conduct tournaments will often have a *tournament director*. Associations with significant tournament activity, such as the USGA, the PGA TOUR, and the LPGA Tour, maintain permanent staff to manage tournaments. In addition, most state and regional golf associations have tournament staffs to manage the hundreds of amateur tournaments they sponsor. Other organizations, such as the American Junior Golf Association, conduct tournaments across the country and frequently post positions for tournament directors. The position of tournament director is described further in Chapter 9.

ADMINISTRATIVE ASSISTANT

There is a great amount of administrative work at associations – from answering the telephone, to proofreading notices, to managing the calendar of a department head. *Administrative assistants* handle these duties. The positions are not glamorous, but are a very standard entrance to careers within an association.

SOUND BITES FROM TOURNAMENT DIRECTORS

Positive

"It's a great way to meet people in the industry."

Negative

"Lots of pressure from deadlines and multiple tasks."

INDUSTRY LEADER Q&A

An interview with Jay Mottola, Executive Director of the Metropolitan Golf Association in Elmsford, N.Y. The Metropolitan Golf Association administers handicapping, course ratings and tournaments for clubs in the New York Metropolitan area and is the governing body of amateur golf in the area with over 450 member clubs.

Q. **What are your duties as executive director?**

A. I'm involved in everything the MGA does without a concentration in any one area. That's one of the great parts of this job. I'm involved with our magazine, *The Met Golfer*, and with our tournament program – but only in an oversight capacity for major events. My primary responsibilities are budgeting and finance; serving as a liaison with other golf organizations; and serving as liaison to our volunteer, elected board of directors.

(continued)

Q. How did you begin your career with the MGA?

A. I started full time in 1980 as tournament director after working part time on the tournament staff in the summers while I was a coach. The MGA's competitions involve from 50 to 100 tournaments a year and the association has always hired teachers, coaches and retirees in the summer to help run them.

Q. What is the most rewarding part of your job?

A. I'm combining a game that I love with work. I see the MGA as a vehicle to serve not just golfers, but also our local community. Through our charitable foundation, we help young people from all segments of society to experience the game. I get a lot satisfaction from that.

Q. What advice do you have for people looking to work in golf associations?

A. There aren't a lot of full-time, high-paying jobs, but the people who do work for associations usually have a deep love of the game and their work. Many people have been here a long time; it's a rewarding career. To get started you need to get your foot in the door. Many people start by doing administrative work as interns or part-timers, and parlay that to full-time positions. There's real potential for successful, creative people.

Q. What kinds of internships are available at the MGA?

A. Our internships are seasonal because of the nature of our services, which include running tournaments, providing a USGA handicap calculation service for our members and rating courses in our area. These services are concentrated during the golf season, from May to October, and we generally hire two or three interns to work in those areas.

Q. **Are there any trends in the industry that are shaping your duties and the role of associations?**

A. Because the services I just mentioned – handicapping, course rating and tournaments – are already established and well run by many associations like the MGA, associations have room to expand their services to their members and their communities. Most golf associations have a charitable foundation, and this is becoming an increasingly important part of what we do. The MGA foundation runs all of our junior programs, our caddie training program and our GOLFWORKS program, which places inner-city kids in summer jobs in the industry. We are always trying to create innovative junior golf programs. They take a lot of time, effort and money to set up, but are a very rewarding part of the job.

CHAPTER THREE

Careers in Facility Development

"The most rewarding aspect of my work is seeing a project rise from a piece of paper into a landscape that people use and use."
Jan Beljan, Senior Designer,
Fazio Golf Course Designers, Inc.

In This Chapter:

- What is a facility?
- What are the types of facilities?
- Why is facility development important?
- What is a golf course developer?
- What is the role of a golf course designer?
- What are the occupations in golf course construction?
- Learn about the following positions:
    Golf Course Architect/Designer
    Building Architect
    Project Manager
    Construction Superintendent
    Irrigation Designer
    Shaper
    Environmental Consultant
- Interview with Jan Beljan, Senior Designer, Fazio Golf Course Designers, Inc.

The last chapter described the associations that provide organization to the industry. Now that you have a broad picture of the industry, our career tour moves to the golf course itself.

The game of golf is inseparable from the courses it is played on. And although golf courses often look like a natural feature of the landscape, dozens of occupations are involved in their development and construction. This chapter will appeal to those who possess vision and creativity and to those who like to work outdoors.

What is a facility?

The term "facility" includes all the buildings and amenities that are a part of a golf course: the pro shop, practice range, clubhouse and sometimes other sports facilities, such as tennis courts. "Facility" and "golf course" are used interchangeably in this book.

What are the trends in golf course development?

The number of U.S. courses has increased greatly the past few years. The number topped 17,000 during the year 2000.

In 2000 and 2001, in excess of 1,500 courses were on the drawing board or under construction (including renovations of existing courses). The National Golf Foundation estimates that by the year 2003, there will be approximately 18,000 courses in the U.S. Of course, no one can predict whether the building boom will continue, but the signs are good.

What are the major types of golf facilities?

Similar positions may have different titles at different types of facilities. On the other hand, two people with the same title may have quite different responsibilities at different facilities. Understanding these differences will help you understand what questions to ask in looking for a position.

There are three broad categories of golf facilities: daily fee, private and municipal.

- The *daily fee* category is the largest with nearly 10,000 golf courses – and comprising approximately 57 percent of all facilities planned or under construction. Daily fee courses are open to the public and charge a fee per round. They sometimes also have annual memberships available for frequent players.

  Within the daily fee category are two major segments: stand-alone courses (without an on-site hotel) and resort golf courses. Both types of daily fee courses may be associated with real estate developments. There are important differences between managing a stand-alone course and a golf resort.

- *Private courses* comprise the second largest category with more than 4,800 courses. Approximately 28 percent of U.S. courses operate as private clubs, but this percentage has been declining. There are two primary types of private clubs: non-equity and equity. Non-equity clubs are typically owned by the developer, an ownership group or a management company, with the members having no ownership interest. This type of private course represents approximately 32 percent of all private golf clubs. Private equity clubs are owned by the members, and they are responsible for all aspects of the club's operation (typically through a board of directors).

  A defining attribute of private clubs is their ability to limit membership. While some private clubs have very large memberships – such as Westchester Country Club in Harrison, N.Y., which hosts PGA TOUR events and has more than 1,000 members – most private clubs have only several hundred. Private clubs may be part of gated communities where only homeowners are eligible for membership. This is explained in more detail later in this chapter.

• In the third category are **municipal** facilities, which represent a little more than 15 percent of all courses. Municipal facilities may be owned by local, county or state governments, and are open to the public. As of June 2001, there were more than 2,700 U.S. municipal facilities.

What is a "regulation" course?

In addition to the three types of facilities described above, there are also different types of courses, which are primarily distinguished by their length. The most common course is a "regulation" course of 18 holes that plays from about 5,200 to 7,200 yards and par of 66 to 72. Some facilities also have a single nine-hole regulation course. Regulation courses conform to standards set by the United States Golf Association, and scores on regulation courses may be entered into the USGA Handicap System.

There are also shorter, non-regulation courses of either 9 or 18 holes, which are sometimes called "executive" or "par-3" courses. Executive courses are generally between 4,000 and 5,200 yards in length, with par between 58 and 65. These courses are comprised primarily of par 3 and par 4 holes, with very few par 5s. Par-3 courses are generally under 4,000 yards in length, comprised of all par 3 holes and have a par of 54 to 57 for 18 holes.

Shorter courses are popular among new golfers and can be an attractive feature of a golf resort. A more recent development is the 2,000 yard course for introducing children to the game.

Why is facility development important?

The development of golf courses is important to your career goals because it is an indicator of industry health. If new courses aren't being built and existing courses become crowded or inaccessible, fewer players will enjoy the game and new players will be discouraged.

If golfers are discouraged from playing, that translates to fewer industry jobs. Of course, if the number of golf courses outpaces the number of golfers, the laws of supply and demand may operate to dampen profits. It will come as no surprise that golf course developers must be willing to bear significant economic risk.

What is a golf course developer?

At the beginning of the golf course cycle is usually the **golf course** *developer*. The developer is the person, company, or municipality that has the vision for creating the golf facility and the financial resources to build it.

Golf courses are expensive to build. Construction costs for an average 18-hole course range from $3 million to $25 million, depending on the quality of the land and other factors. A word of caution: It may be unrealistic to set your sights on becoming a developer because the field is competitive and carries great financial risk. There are, however, many other careers within the development sector, listed below.

Financial analysts working with developers run financial projections to determine whether land will provide a sound investment return as a golf facility, or if it should be developed for some other use, such as a shopping mall or office complex, or perhaps just sold.

Also involved in the investment decision will be a *golf course designer* or *architect* to provide preliminary design and cost projections. This position is described more fully in the second half of this chapter.

The developer and designer will check with **environmental consultants** and **environmental engineers** to determine how to conform to environmental regulations and obtain building permits. *Construction engineers* also may be called in.

Computer technology specialists are increasingly important in the design and construction of courses. Two technologies have had major impact: Global Positioning Systems or GPS, which use satellites to capture geographical and geological information previously obtained by expensive surveying and soil testing; and Computer Assisted Design, or CAD, which allows designers to evaluate myriad designs and construction costs before construction begins. Using CAD, a designer can determine how many cubic feet of earth must be moved to create hills or other land forms. The software is also able to calculate the time and cost of construction.

Once the decision is made to build a course and a final design is confirmed, the developer will hire a *construction contractor*. Or the developer may have an in-house construction staff.

What are the different types of developers?

- *Real estate and investment developers* are the most common golf course developers today. About 150 acres of land are needed for an average 18-hole course — more if the land is environmentally sensitive. Given the sheer acreage of a golf course and the building and zoning permits required, it is easy to understand why golf developers are closely allied with the real estate business.

(For a comprehensive description of golf course development, read the Urban Land Institute's *How to Develop a Successful Golf-Oriented Community*. For more information call 800-321-5011. Also check the National Golf Foundation publications at www.ngf. org.)

The real estate developer is motivated by profits derived from selling homes around a course, by selling the golf course and clubhouse once they are built, or by collecting members' fees or green fees.

It is increasingly common for developers to manage their courses after development. Developers who manage a portfolio of courses are referred to as *management companies*, which are described in the next chapter.

A good way to discover opportunities is to review the employment and job opportunity pages on developers' Web sites.

Here are a few prominent developers with good Web sites:
- ➢ Landmark Golf Company: www.landmarkgolf.com
- ➢ Toll Brothers: www.tollbrothers.com
- ➢ Taylor Woodrow Communities: www.taylorwoodrow.com

- *Municipal developers:* Municipalities develop golf facilities as part of a community's recreational plan. Because a municipality usually owns the land, its economic analysis will focus on how much construction and maintenance will cost taxpayers and whether a golf course is a good use of land and money. *City planners* may be consulted to help make that decision, along with golf course designers and contractors.

  Once built, the golf course may be managed by the municipality's recreation and parks department, or the municipality may contract with a management company (described in the next chapter) to oversee the entire operation.

  There are some very famous municipal courses. The 2002 U.S. Open is scheduled to be played at Bethpage State Park, a public course on Long Island operated by the State of New York.

  If working for municipal courses interests you, take a look at colleges that offer degrees in recreation management. Also see the National Recreation and Park Association's Web site, www.nrpa.org.

- *Golf-enthusiast developers:* A golf course also may be developed by a group of individuals who have the vision and resources to build their own course. These courses, generally private, are built for the pleasure of the game and not for expectation of profit. The investors contract with developers for design and construction. Famous private courses, such as Augusta National, site of The Masters, and Pine Valley in New Jersey, which is consistently rated the top course in the U.S., were both developed by golf enthusiasts.

- *Not-for-profit developer:* A new type of developer is emerging in the golf industry. Unused land – even in urban settings – is being developed by not-for-profits, such as The First Tee, www.thefirsttee.org. The First Tee helps build golf facilities for young people who don't have access to the game. The First Tee provides local communities with business planning, design and construction assistance, financial grants and fundraising support. The First Tee has the support of major golf associations and businesses.

Who designs golf courses?

Most courses are designed by either an architect or designer. The term "architect" is usually reserved for those with degrees in landscape architecture, a specialty within civil engineering – not to be confused with traditional building architecture. The term "designer" refers to anyone who designs courses, regardless of their background or training. Famous golfers, such as Arnold Palmer, Jack Nicklaus, Nancy Lopez and Jan Stephenson have become golf course designers.

What is irrigation design?

Today's designers commonly work very closely with *irrigation consultants and designers* during both the design and construction process. In fact, often hanging on the wall next to the architect's course design is the irrigation design.

Although most golfers notice only sprinkler heads on the fairway, the underlying irrigation infrastructure is a complex system that collects water and recycles it back to the course. Positions in the irrigation field are explored in the second half of this chapter.

What other occupations are involved in building golf courses?

When a course is ready to be built, a developer hires a *construction contractor* – although some developers have in-house construction companies. The developer, construction company and designer work together throughout construction.

Throughout construction the developer usually has an on-site representative, often called a *project manager* or *director of construction*. The *general manager* of the facility may also be on site.

Meanwhile, a *construction or project superintendent* working for the construction company will supervise the building of the course. It is common for a construction company to subcontract some aspects of construction, such as installation of irrigation and pump stations, landscaping and paving projects.

Many different crews will be working on different things at the same time. For example, cart paths will be paved around greens that are still being built. Irrigation trenches will be dug while lakes and ponds are still being carved. Fairways, in turn, will be in different stages of shaping.

Those in the construction side of the industry enjoy the creativity, but quickly point out the strain on family life that results from moving from project to project.

Where will I find more information about golf design and construction?

Here are a few leads to find out more about golf design and construction:

➢ The American Society of Golf Course Architects: www.asgca.org.

➢ The Golf Course Builders Association of America, www.gcbaa.org, supports the golf course construction industry. Its Web site lists more than 100 construction companies and other companies that supply the building industry. If you know a builder, consider asking if you could be their guest at the GCBAA annual meeting.

➢ The Irrigation Association, www.irrigation.org, provides services to a variety of irrigation occupations, from irrigation of farms to golf courses. They also offer educational seminars.

➢ The American Society of Irrigation Consultants, www.asic.org, specializes in turf grass and includes a list of consultants across the country.

➢ The Golf Course Superintendents Association of America, www.gcsaa.org, provides education and services to thousands of golf course superintendents. Although GCSAA members are mostly involved in maintaining existing courses, their knowledge and research is invaluable to the "grow-in" stage of new golf courses.

➢ Also see National Golf Foundation publications on golf course development and construction: www.ngf.org.

All three of the large construction companies listed below include employment opportunities on their Web sites, which are good sources of information about the duties and requirements of construction jobs. Look for construction companies with training programs if you are looking for an entry-level position.

➢ Landcapes Unlimited, Inc.: www.landscapesunlimited.com
➢ Ryangolf: www.ryangolf.com
➢ Wadsworth Golf Construction Company: www.wadsworthgolf.com

CAREERS TO EXPLORE

Career Close-up: GOLF COURSE ARCHITECT/DESIGNER

You may have heard a golfer say, "This tee is in the wrong place," or

JOB HUNTING TIPS:
Contact the local
GCSAA chapter

How do you find a job working in golf course construction or maintenance? One of the best routes is to contact the local chapter of the Golf Course Superintendents Association of America through their Web site www.gcsaa.org. Local chapters know what courses are under construction and whom to contact. They also will be able to provide a list of courses that may be hiring maintenance workers.

Or you can inquire directly with the manager of a local golf course. If you do not know how to get in touch with courses in your area, check the Web site of your local state golf association or find the local associations through the USGA Web site www.usga.org.

Another resource is the Golf Course Builders Association of America: www.gcbaa.org.

"This bunker should be moved." In fact, most golfers at one time or another have designed or re-designed a course in their minds.

But it is impossible for most golfers to envision how much work goes into course design. They don't see how much earth was moved or the extensive drainage below the surface. Nor do they understand the increasing environmental considerations involved. The true role of an *architect* or *designer* is not well understood.

DUTIES: A designer's initial duty is to analyze the land, studying topography, drainage, environmental challenges and general suitability for the course that the developer has envisioned.

In the next phase, the designer "routes" the course and suggests where tees, fairways and greens will be placed. Routing is a critical design stage that determines how the course will relate to the site's topography.

After the preliminary layout is approved, the designer finalizes specifications for fairways and greens. Working with irrigation consultants and engineers, the designer will make sure the irrigation design works with the course design. The designer also will be involved in obtaining building and zoning permits and meeting environmental regulations.

As design plans are finalized, the budget is revised. The project will then be submitted for bids from construction contractors or turned over to an in-house construction company. With contracts in place, the designer supervises construction.

SALARY RANGE: A design associate beginning his or her career in an established design firm earns approximately $35,000 annually. Self-employed, entry-level designers will earn less until they establish their reputations and client bases. With five years experience, annual salaries approach $75,000. Highly sought-after designers with their own firms earn the top incomes in the industry.

JOB OPPORTUNITIES: Although the field is competitive, opportunities remain good. There is always room for talented designers, with renovations of older courses filling the gap when new course construction is at a lull.

EDUCATION & TRAINING: There is no specific course of study to become a golf course designer. One path of formal education involves a major in landscape architecture or agronomy. While studying agronomy, many students also take courses in golf course design.

Another career path involves on-the-job experience in course construction, combined with an extensive knowledge of the game. Prospective golf course designers are urged to work on a maintenance crew or a construction crew before beginning formal training. Computer skills are also essential: Course design and construction has changed dramatically over the last decade with the introduction of Computer Assisted Design (CAD) and Global Positioning Systems (GPS).

ENTRY-LEVEL POSITIONS: Assistant or junior designers are entry-level jobs. These positions are available to those with formal training or construction and maintenance experience. Some design firms offer apprenticeships.

GOLF ABILITY & INTEREST: In order to design a course of quality, the designer should be a proficient golfer. Otherwise, he or she will not be able to design a course that is challenging to the scratch golfer or tour professional. It is also important to be familiar with many different types of courses

SPECIAL SKILLS & PERSONAL TRAITS: Good communication skills rank high because a designer must coordinate many competing interests. Golf course construction requires the approval of planning and zoning boards, which may ask for revised plans and financial projections. As one top designer says, "The designer must be flexible, creative and persuasive."

CAREER LADDER & PROMOTION PROSPECTS: Promotions within a design firm generally proceed from assistant or junior designer to senior designer. A career goal may be to head one's own firm.

ARCHITECT – CLUBHOUSE AND OTHER STRUCTURES

A golf facility also includes a clubhouse and other buildings. Some architectural firms specialize in designing clubhouses, maintenance buildings and practice range facilities.

Becoming a *building architect* generally involves a five-year college program, plus an internship with a firm. If you do not want to become an architect, but would still like to work on golf course buildings, consider becoming a *draftsman* or a *computer technician* specializing in architectural computer programs. Then look for a position with an architectural firm that specializes in the construction of golf facilities.

PROJECT MANAGER

A key employee of the developer – and the construction company – is the *project manager*. He or she is responsible for keeping all of the pieces on track, including overseeing the bidding process and hiring construction supervisors. The project also could include a clubhouse

JOB HUNTING TIPS:
Seek out designers' Web sites
Use an Internet search engine to find "golf course designers and architects." Many designers have their own Web sites, which are filled with information about golf course design. If you are firmly committed to the design profession, contact a developer and inquire about internships.

and residential properties, which may require working with a sales and marketing department.

The project manager is more apt to work in an office (probably in a temporary trailer) surrounded by budgets and time lines, than on the course itself.

Extensive experience in golf course construction is required for project management, along with good business judgment and communication skills.

Educational background varies. Some project managers have college degrees in landscape architecture, turf management or business, but others entered construction directly from high school and have worked their way through the ranks.

Our research identified the following colleges as having good programs for construction management:

➤ Lake City Community College, Lake City, Fla: www.lakecity.cc.fl.us
➤ Mississippi State University, Starkville, Miss.: www.msstate.edu
➤ North Carolina State University, Raleigh, N.C.: www.ncsu.edu
➤ Texas Tech University, Lubbock, Texas: www.ttu.edu
➤ University of Nebraska-Lincoln, Lincoln, Neb.: www.unl.edu

CONSTRUCTION SUPERINTENDENT

Daily supervision of the construction crew rests with the *construction superintendent* – also called a *job* or *project superintendent*.

A construction superintendent is significantly different from the golf course superintendent described in the Chapter 5 – Careers in Turf Management. Specific construction knowledge – managing large earth-moving equipment and installing pump stations – is a major part of course construction and is the responsibility of the construction superintendent, not the golf course superintendent. Construction superintendents frequently have oversight for the "growing-in" stage of a new course. Most important, construction superintendents constantly move from project to project, while course superintendents can expect to work at the same facility for years.

It is the construction superintendent who "OKs" construction at critical stages and makes sure it conforms with design and building standards. Golfers take for granted that tees are flat, that puddles don't form on cart paths, and that greens are built to USGA specifications. But at each stage, the construction superintendent must approve the work, and solid knowledge of the way the game is played is critical.

Education for a construction superintendent varies. A background in construction or turf management is helpful, but on-the-job experience remains critical. Communication skills and the ability to lead a team through months of coordinated efforts are also important. As one construction superintendent put it, "Most of the things we do, you can't learn in a classroom."

Another plus is that this occupation can be a springboard to many other jobs. Construction superintendents often work in sales for manufacturers of construction, turf maintenance or irrigation equipment.

The annual salary range is $40,000 to $60,000, plus travel and living expenses and company benefits.

IRRIGATION DESIGNER

A few decades ago, most *irrigation designers* worked for manufacturers or distributors of irrigation equipment. The trend, however, is for irrigation systems to be designed by independent irrigation designers who bid a project out to manufacturers or course architects.

This has changed the career path for irrigation designers. Whereas experience on an irrigation installation crew, or in the sales department of a manufacturer of irrigation equipment were once standard entry positions, an irrigation designer is now more likely to need formal education in agricultural engineering, landscape architecture (civil engineering), or golf course construction management.

The Irrigation Association, www.irrigation.org, offers a certification program with a sub-specialty in golf. The certificate can lead to entry-level positions with an irrigation design firm, irrigation equipment distributor, irrigation installation company or course maintenance crew.

Irrigation installation is a field separate from irrigation design. The typical stages of an installation project involve digging trenches, laying an extensive system of pipes and drains, and then returning the ground to the form the architect envisioned. Lake City Community College in Lake City, Fla., www.lakecity.cc.fl.us, offers one of the few two-year associate degrees in *irrigation management*.

The manufacturers of irrigation equipment also offer training and education programs. Three large irrigation equipment manufacturers are:

- ➢ The Toro Company: www.toro.com
- ➢ Rain Bird Sales, Inc.: www.rainbird.com
- ➢ Hunter Golf: www.huntergolf.com

Some construction projects hire an *irrigation superintendent* to manage installation. As with many occupations in golf construction, extensive travel is involved as irrigation crews move from project to project. Knowledge of golf is helpful, but far less important in installation than in irrigation system design.

Golf course irrigation is just one aspect of a larger profession. For a broad view of the irrigation industry, check the Irrigation Association's Web site, www.irrigation.org. Mid-career opportunities in golf exist for those working in residential or agricultural irrigation. Consult the Web sites mentioned earlier in the chapter for more information.

SHAPER

More than 50 different types of construction equipment are used to build a course. Most machine operators need little golf knowledge to do their jobs well. An exception is the occupation of *shaper*. Experienced shapers are in high demand.

If you like operating earth-moving machinery and understand golf, you might consider the interesting career of shaper. The shaper operates a specialized shaping machine (like a bulldozer but with smaller, more maneuverable blades) and moves earth to create the topographical surface indicated in a designer's plan.

For example, the designer's blueprint may show a fairway bordered by 10-foot mounds. Dump trucks and dozers will move thousands of cubic feet of dirt to approximate mound positions on the fairway's edge. The shaper then moves the earth to achieve the required elevations. In so doing, he or she exercises a great deal of judgment (and machinery expertise).

The average salary for experienced shapers is approximately $70,000 annually, but shapers willing to work overseas can earn as much as $200,000 per year. These figures include housing benefits. Most shapers begin their occupation by working on a construction crew.

ENVIRONMENTAL CONSULTANT

Many of the classic courses built decades ago could not be built today because of current environmental regulations. No discussion of golf course construction would be complete without mentioning careers in environmental science. (Environmental issues are also covered in Chapter 5 – Careers in Turf Management).

Environmental consultants are brought in early in facility development to advise on the permits needed for construction. Many consultants have college degrees in environmental science or in civil engineering, but there is no sub-specialty for golf.

➤ If you are interested in environmental issues, you may find Audubon International, www.audubonintl.org, programs interesting. In 1991, Audubon International established the Audubon Cooperative Sanctuary Program for Golf Courses. More than 2,000 courses in the U.S. and Canada have met the certification requirements of the program. The organization is hopeful that a new occupation will emerge at courses – that of ***natural resource manager***. Perhaps you will be on the cutting edge of this career. For more information, contact the Audubon Cooperative Sanctuary office at 518-767-9051.

➤ Another environmental resource is the Green Section of the USGA, www.usga.org.

INDUSTRY LEADER Q&A

An interview with Jan Beljan, Senior Designer, Fazio Golf Course Designers, Inc., located in Jupiter, Fla.

Q. **How did you decide on your career after a few years in the industry?**

A. Landscape architecture offered the gamut – the creative, the artistic, as well as landscape design, turf science and graphic design.

Q. **What people skills are needed in your client-oriented business?**

A. You have to be able to convey messages verbally and graphically. Clients often have their own ideas – and they may be good ideas – but you may find there's a better way to do it. It's my job to convey the disadvantages of the clients' proposals without being too negative and to find the positives and build on them.

Q. **What's the hardest thing about your job?**

A. The weather – it's an unknown. You can't count on anything. It may rain too much or not enough. Wind impacts construction as does excessive heat or cold.

Q. **What's the most rewarding aspect of your work?**

A. Seeing a project rise from a piece of paper into a landscape that people use and use. I'm proud of all my jobs

(continued)

because they're collaborative efforts – with concessions made by the developer, the owner and the designer.

Q. What are you most proud of?

A. The way the courses are maintained. The clients are very good about maintaining the integrity of the design through their commitment to good golf course maintenance.

Q. How has the role of women changed over the years in your field?

A. There are more women in it now, but it's a difficult field for both women and men. It's a difficult job, and it's difficult to break into course design. It takes a huge commitment of time and energy. It's sometimes about being in the right place at the right time.

Q. What's the best educational path to careers in golf course development?

A. Studying landscape architecture is a proven avenue to acquiring the right skills, and you can branch into horticulture and agronomy. The more well-rounded you are, the more insight you have. It helps to work on a grounds crew to understand the man hours required to maintain a course or to be on a construction crew to see the process of building a course.

Q. How important is it to be able to play the game well?

A. You don't need to play it well, but you must understand the game and that there are many types of golf courses. They must be playable by and interesting for a wide range of players. They also need to be functional for those operating and maintaining them, as well as aesthetically pleasing to all.

Q. What makes a good course?

A. There's a lot of science, but also a lot of art. It's the melding of the two. You can have the art without the science, and the appeal may not last very long. The course may become predictable in a bad way – like when you know that a well struck shot may put you in a hazard instead of offering the reward of a better position to play the next shot.

CHAPTER FOUR

Careers in Facility Management

"If you enjoy working with people, leading teams and watching your efforts unfold on a daily basis, then golf management is a great place to be. It's a people-intensive environment. You get feedback every day, every hour. That's addictive."

David Pillsbury, Co-President & CEO,
American Golf Corporation

In This Chapter:

- What is the role of the general manager?
- How does management differ at different types of facilities?
- Who works for the general manager?
- What is a golf management company?
- What are some staff opportunites?
- Learn about the following positions:
    - General Manager – Daily Fee Course
    - General Manager – Resort Course
    - General Manager – Private Club
    - General Manager – Municipal Course
    - Director of Golf
    - Food and Beverage Director
- Interview with David Pillsbury, Co-President & CEO, American Golf Corporation

In the previous chapter we toured outdoor occupations – designing and building golf courses. Now our tour moves indoors. This chapter focuses on managing facilities that are ready for customers. If you like providing customer service, you may find your occupation in this segment.

Why is management important?

A golf course may be in perfect condition, but the ultimate success of a facility will depend on how it is managed and how the staff interprets "customer service." This is especially true at a golf resort, where a customer's experience extends beyond the course to hotel rooms, restaurants and other amenities.

A positive off-course experience enhances the likelihood that a golfer will return to a course or resort. That is why good managers are always in demand. If you like management responsibilities, you will find excellent opportunities in this sector.

One of the benefits of working at a facility is access to the golf course. Although work and play don't always mix, many facilities allow off-duty employees to play golf at non-peak times.

What is the top management position at a golf facility?

The top management position at most facilities is the *general manager* – often called the "GM." At a large facility the GM usually reports to the chief executive officer or owner. If a facility is owned and operated by a management company (described later in this chapter), the general manager may report to a corporate or regional executive. At small facilities, the general manager may also be the owner. At other facilities, the *director of golf* has a role similar to that of a general manager.

What does the general manager do?

Most facilities divide the operation of the facility between the maintenance of the golf course and "everything else." The general manager manages "everything else." In a large golf resort, that could mean overseeing hundreds of employees.

The GM is usually responsible for the retail shop, range, instruction programs, restaurant and catering facilities, locker rooms, service buildings, hotel and conference rooms, and other sports facilities. Being a GM is a big job.

Effective managers are like good team captains. They know what plays to call and when and how to get the most from their employees. Many books have been written about the difference between management and leadership skills, but the bottom line is that good general managers get high marks in both.

Who works for the general manager?

The general manager may have a large or small staff depending on the size of the facility. The GM of an 18-hole municipal course with a small pro shop and coffee shop may have only a few shop assistants and one assistant overseeing the food and beverage operations.

At the other extreme, the general manager of a large resort may have a dozen department heads reporting to him or her – including a *food and beverage manager* and a director of golf (reviewed in the second half of this chapter).

Who is the GM's boss?

The general manager often reports to two – sometimes competing – bosses. The first is the owner or Board of Directors; they are interested in profits. The second is the customer, who expects excellent service and value regardless of profits to the owner. The responsibilities of the general manager have much to do with the expectations of customers.

In the long run, the most profitable facilities are those that best serve their customers. But in the short run, general managers are often under pressure to cut corners and meet their budgets.

What is a golf management company?

One trend in the industry is the growth of companies specializing in managing many courses – either their own or those owned by others. Management companies seek economic efficiencies and increased revenues resulting from consolidation. One advantage of working for a course operated by a management company is the opportunity for promotion to its corporate management.

Some management companies manage only a few courses. Others, like the American Golf Corporation, www.americangolf.com, manage hundreds. Some management companies specialize in a specific type of facility. For example, ClubCorp, www.clubcorp.com, is a highly respected manager of primarily private clubs.

Crittenden Golf, a publisher of golf newsletters and magazines, has an annual *Directory of Golf Management Companies*, available for $287. For information see www.crittendengolf.com.

The July 2001 issue of Crittenden's Golf Inc. magazine lists the following management companies as the largest according to the number of courses. Each company has a Web site that explains its mission and structure, as well as employment opportunities:

> ➤ American Golf Corporation: www.americangolf.com
> ➤ ClubCorp: www.clubcorp.com
> ➤ Meadowbrook Golf Group: www.mggi.com
> ➤ Troon Golf Management: www.troongolf.com
> ➤ KemperSports Management: www.kempersports.com
> ➤ Evergreen Alliance Golf Ltd.: www.eaglgolf.com

Are there non-management positions?

Not everyone is cut out to be a manager. Some of us do not like telling other people what to do. We prefer to simply do our own job.

If that describes you, consider working in one of the many staff positions at a golf facility. You may enjoy working in a restaurant but would rather work at a golf course restaurant. Or you may enjoy working behind the counter in a retail position, but prefer to sell golf apparel.

If you take one of these positions, you may surprise yourself and find that you are comfortable supervising others and be promoted to a management position.

Where can I learn more about facility management?

Professional golf instructor programs, such as those offered by The PGA of America, www.pga.com, and the LPGA, www.lpga.com, include courses on management.

In addition, the National Golf Foundation co-sponsors an annual National Institute of Golf Management program for people already employed in the industry. For more information, visit www.ngf.org.

The Club Managers Association of America, www.cmaa.org, operates many management training programs for all types of clubs. In order to enroll, applicants must be sponsored by an employer. An entry-level position at a golf or even non-golf facility will offer the opportunity to take a CMAA seminar or certification program. When interviewing for a position, you may want to inquire whether the facility is a member of the CMAA, and whether it sponsors promising employees for CMAA study.

The National Club Association, www.natlclub.org, serves private clubs. Its publications – the list is available on the Web site – cover club management topics and are available to non-members. Of particular interest is *Model Job Descriptions for Key Club Personnel* ($69 for non-members).

Another helpful source is the hotel industry. Many large hotel companies, such as the Marriott Corporation, www.marriott.com, have management training programs. These programs are often open to college graduates who have an interest in the hospitality industry.

And remember to check general employment Web sites, such as www.hotjobs.com and www.monster.com. Look for club manager or food and beverage positions. The job descriptions will help you decide whether this is a career path for you.

CAREERS TO EXPLORE

Career Close-up: GENERAL MANAGER – DAILY FEE GOLF COURSE

DUTIES: The primary responsibility of the *general manager* of a daily fee course is to keep an operation running efficiently and smoothly. Since the GM can't be everywhere, he or she must hire managers for different departments. Some managers delegate tremendous responsibility to their senior staff, while others stay closely involved in the daily supervision of activities.

A major portion of the general manager's time is spent communicating with and motivating his or her staff.

SALARY RANGE: An entry-level manager of a small facility earns about $30,000 annually. Experienced general managers at large facilities average closer to $52,000 per year. A manager of a top facility may earn well above $80,000. Salaries in the Sun Belt (southern half of the U.S.) are generally higher than in the Frost Belt (source: National Golf Foundation).

JOB OPPORTUNITIES: Good managers are becoming increasingly valuable as the industry booms and competition increases.

EDUCATION & TRAINING: There are several career paths to becoming a general manager at a daily-fee facility.

- **General college education:** A college degree with a business major is highly recommended. Related work experience or internships should be an integral part of your education.

- **Experience:** People who have managed restaurants, clubs or sports facilities can move to a golf facility. It helps to have some golf knowledge.

- **Special certificate programs:** Once you have demonstrated management ability at a golf facility, you can take advantage of certificate programs offered by the Club Managers Association of America.

- **Golf professional programs:** The PGA of America, www.pga.com, and LPGA, www.lpga.com, include courses on facility management in their certification programs (described in Chapter 8). Many PGA and LPGA professionals are promoted to general manager from the position of director of golf.

- **Promotion from other fields:** A final, though less common, avenue is to be promoted to general manager from the position of golf course superintendent.

ENTRY-LEVEL POSITIONS: Any position that offers an opportunity to understand golfers' needs and habits is helpful. Once you have demonstrated managerial skills – in whichever department – promotion opportunities are likely to become available. Following are several traditional entry-level positions: ***pro shop assistant***, ***cart attendant***, ***assistant superintendent***, ***assistant manager***, and ***staff positions*** in restaurant or catering departments.

GOLF ABILITY & INTEREST: Managers who have a role in marketing a golf course for outings or potential members may need to do some "selling" during rounds of golf. A low handicap can be a plus. Most managers report, however, that they seldom get a chance to play.

SPECIAL SKILLS & PERSONAL TRAITS: Managers must have strong people skills. If you like to sit alone in an office and review budgets, you probably would not enjoy a management career. If you would rather plan and teach golf, management may not be for you either.

People skills are important because the hiring and training of employees is often a major duty. Computer skills are also important, especially in finance and accounting departments. Finally, managers are often required to react quickly to emergencies – from employee disputes to problems on the course. The manager must be decisive – and a good problem solver.

CAREER LADDER & PROMOTION PROSPECTS: Most general managers were promoted from assistant manager positions. A good track record as a manager or assistant manager at golf facility can also lead to an executive position with a golf management company.

GENERAL MANAGER – GOLF RESORT

The number of golf resorts has grown over the last decade as large hotel chains have added courses to their amenities. The duties of a general manager of a full golf resort – with hotel and conference facilities – are broader than the duties of a manager at a traditional daily fee facility. A large golf resort may have up to 1,000 employees. Generally, golf facilities are managed separately from hotel functions.

The starting point to becoming a general manager need not be a position in golf. Positions in restaurant or hotel operations, marketing departments, and conference and catering facilities are also good entry-level jobs. Most resort GMs suggest that the best training is to work in a variety of resort operations, starting from the bottom up.

Although golf knowledge is important, general managers may not play often. Management skills are more important than golf skills.

GENERAL MANAGER – PRIVATE CLUB

The general manager of a private equity club is in a unique position because every member is an owner. The manager may sometimes feel as though he or she reports to dozens – or hundreds – of bosses.

Private golf clubs traditionally pay top salaries to general managers in order to ensure that members receive top service. Entry-level posi-

---

JOB HUNTING TIPS:

Read management books

Check the management section of a bookstore and select a book or two on "How to Be a Manager." Even though they are not written specifically for the golf industry, they provide good background on what a manager does.

tions in golf course or food and beverage operations provide good experience.

It is sometimes difficult to find a list of private clubs in your area. You may find a listing on the web site of your state golf association.

GENERAL MANAGER – MUNICIPAL COURSE

Managers of municipal golf facilities are usually employed by recreation and parks departments and report to local elected officials. Although municipal facilities are accountable to taxpayers, the facilities are not generally profit-driven. There is also less focus on marketing since the customer base is established. Some municipal managers have been promoted from positions as golf instructors; others have been promoted from management positions within a recreation department.

DIRECTOR OF GOLF

At most golf facilities the ***director of golf*** is primarily in charge of the golf operations with little – if anything – to do with the food and beverage operations.

In recent years, however, as the golf industry has expanded, directors of golf have experienced increased opportunity for career advancement. A highly motivated and experienced director of golf may be asked to take on responsibility for the food and beverage operations along with other departments. The Professional Golf Management programs described in Chapter 8 – Player Instruction prepare golf professionals for management positions.

> **SOUND BITES FROM GENERAL MANAGERS**
> **Positive**
> "You get to go to the golf course every day!"
> **Negative**
> "It's tough on family life in the middle of the season."
> "We play less golf than people think."

Career Close-up: FOOD AND BEVERAGE DIRECTOR

DUTIES: The ***food and beverage director*** is responsible for all dining facilities and catering operations, including the kitchen design and equipment. The ***chef*** and ***catering director*** report to the food and beverage director.

SALARY RANGE: The median annual salary of the F&B director at a daily fee facility is approximately $30,000 (source: National Golf Foundation). Salaries are significantly higher in private clubs and large resorts.

JOB OPPORTUNITIES: Job opportunities are excellent for those with good track records. Facilities look for F&B directors who understand how to maximize profits and meet customer expectations.

EDUCATION & TRAINING: There are three basic paths into food and beverage careers. One experienced manager estimates that 60 percent of F&B managers at golf facilities previously worked as *hotel F&B managers or assistant managers*. (Hotels often have excellent management training programs.) According to our survey, about 25 percent of F&B managers began as chefs. The remaining percentage graduated from professional golf schools. The Club Managers Association of America, www.cmaa.org, has many training programs to help F&B managers advance in their careers.

ENTRY-LEVEL POSITIONS: A typical career path might include positions as a waiter, head waiter, dining room supervisor, and then, finally, food and beverage manager. Even a position as a dishwasher can be leveraged into better opportunities. No matter where you start, most managers value hard workers who understand customer service.

GOLF ABILITY & INTEREST: Food and beverage managers do not generally consider golf skills as important to their jobs. But most say that it helps to play and understand the game. At an active club with more than 1,500 families, as many as 800 meals a day may be served; it helps to like golfers when you are serving so many of them.

SPECIAL SKILLS & PERSONAL TRAITS: People skills are critical, whether for managing employees or making sure customers are properly served. To get ahead in the F&B industry, be prepared to work long hours. Unlike traditional restaurants, most golf facilities are seasonal. That means months of grueling hours with the reward of a few slow months in the off-season.

INDUSTRY LEADER Q&A

An interview with David Pillsbury, Co-President & CEO, American Golf Corporation, located in Santa Monica, Calif., which manages over 320 private, resort and daily fee courses in the U.S., United Kingdom and Australia.

Q. **How did you get into the golf industry?**

A. I'd only played golf about 15 times before going into the business. I worked for Mattel, Inc. toy company and attended an executive MBA program at USC on weekends. Between my first and second year in the program, I met Joe Guerra from American Golf Corp. Every weekend

I'd sit next to Joe, and he'd tell me what an incredible future there was in the golf industry. I wanted to marry my professional career aspirations with my personal values. I felt that golf was where they came together.

Q. **What was your first job in golf?**

A. I started as a manager trainee with American Golf Corp, which meant I was starting at an entry-level position. It was gritty, hard work, but fulfilling. You're a significant part of something that's important to people.

Q. **What would you tell someone interested in working in golf facility management?**

A. If you like to compartmentalize your life and go home at 5 p.m., this is not the place for you. It's a lifestyle; it becomes who you are. The lines between your recreational life, work life and personal life are blurred. It takes a significant personal commitment, but has rich rewards.

Q. **What's the best part of working in your field?**

A. If you enjoy working with people, leading teams and watching your efforts unfold daily, then golf facility management is a great place to be. It's also a very people-intensive environment. When you're at a facility, you get feedback every day, every hour. It's addictive.

Q. **What do you look for in the people you hire for entry-level positions?**

A. For manager trainees, we prefer people with some hospitality experience. We do bring people into the business who don't have golf backgrounds, but who do have all the personal attributes to become leaders.

SOUND BITES FROM FOOD & BEVERAGE MANAGERS

"Chefs are the stars, but behind the scenes are the managers."

(continued)

Q. Is it necessary to have some kind of certification to work in facility management?

A. While it is preferable to be a PGA or LPGA pro or have other certification, we do have extensive training that everyone goes through. It's important that non-golfers not be discouraged; I'm an example of what's possible.

Q. What's the career outlook for your field?

A. Great people are always needed; there's no shortage of opportunities for them.

CHAPTER FIVE

Careers in Turf Management

"When your office is the great outdoors, what's not to love?"
> Scott Woodhead, Golf Operations Manager,
> Heart River Golf Course and past president
> of the Golf Course Superintendents
> Association of America

In This Chapter:

- What are some occupations in turf management?
- What types of education and training are available?
- Is college necessary?
- Why is working on a crew important?
- Learn about the following positions:
    - Golf Course Superintendent
    - Assistant Golf Course Superintendent
    - Irrigation Specialist
    - Equipment Manager
- Interview with Scott Woodhead, Golf Operations Manager, Heart River Golf Course and past president of the Golf Course Superintendents Association of America

At this point in our career journey, a developer has invested millions to build a course and hire a management team. Hopefully, golfers are using the course.

Now comes the real test: Will golfers find that course conditions meet their expectations? Will they enjoy their round enough to return? The answers to those questions rest on careers in turf management. The turf management sector plays an important role in the financial health of a golf course.

What is "turf?"

To the average golfer, the word "turf" means soil, grass, or simply the golf course, and turf management involves keeping the course in excellent condition.

But within the golf industry, turf management has a broader meaning. It involves much more than mowing fairways and greens. It may involve draining and cleaning ponds and lakes and making sure the pumping station for the course irrigation system is working correctly. It may involve understanding different types of maintenance equipment and keeping them in top working order. It may involve determining the best type of grasses for particular soil and weather conditions.

What is the GCSAA?

It is impossible to discuss turf management without mentioning the work of the Golf Course Superintendents Association of America – or GCSAA.

Since its founding in 1926, the GCSAA has worked hard to set professional standards and raise the profile of the turf management industry. It sponsors an annual trade show with more than 20,000 attendees and 700 exhibitors, and conducts numerous seminars for its nearly 22,000 members. The GCSAA also provides job placement and career services to members.

The GCSAA is supported by a network of local chapters, which are easy to identify through the chapter section of the GCSAA's very helpful Web site, www.gcsaa.org. Do not hesitate to contact your local chapter for information about career information or job opportunities.

The GCSAA offers student memberships to turf management majors. Portions of their monthly publication, *Golf Course Management*, are available online to non-members. If you contact your local chapter of GCSAA or know a superintendent, you may be able to obtain copies of GCSAA publications. They provide excellent insights into the turf management industry.

Another good resource is the GCSAA's *College Guide*, which has information on tuition, financial aid, internships, research projects and application processes for more than 100 colleges in the U.S. It also includes information about international programs. The guide can be ordered for $20 through the GCSAA's service center at 800-472-7878.

What kinds of positions are available in turf management?

If you like working outdoors around golfers, there probably is a career waiting for you in turf management. Positions are varied – from **mechanic** to **manager**. The education needed ranges from one-year program certifications to graduate degrees in agronomy. Turf management is one of the most dynamic sectors in the industry and offers great opportunities.

Following are the key positions in turf management: **Golf course superintendent**, **assistant golf course superintendent**, **equipment manager**, **assistant equipment manager**, **horticulturist** and **irrigation specialist**.

In addition, there are often staff positions as **chemical technicians** (pesticide management), *irrigation technicians* and *equipment operators*.

How do I find a position on a maintenance crew?

One of the best ways to determine whether you would like working in turf management is to work on a maintenance crew. The experience is excellent preparation for advanced study.

Here are several ways to find entry-level postions:

➢ Check with your local GCSAA chapter (explained above) to find facilities looking for workers.

➢ Visit golf employment Web sites and search for "technician" or "equipment operator" in the turf sector. Although most jobs require experience, you may find some with entry-level training. There is one Web site devoted entirely to turf jobs, www.turfnet.com.

➢ Search employment Web sites for internships in turf management. An internship assumes that applicants have little prior experience.

➢ Obtain a list of courses in your area and call superintendents to inquire about openings. Be sure to follow up by sending a résumé.

➢ Ask your high school to establish an alliance with a local course or GCSAA chapter. Even if internships are not available, superintendents are often willing to speak about their duties with students.

> **JOB HUNTING TIPS:**
>
> **Attend a trade show**
>
> The GCSAA sponsors an annual trade show for the turf management industry, usually in mid-February. If you know someone in the industry, they may be able to bring you as their guest. The GCSAA maintains an electronic job-posting system at the show for all attendees.
>
> The major manufacturers of turf equipment also maintain employment pages on their Web sites. Following are the sites of three major manufacturers: www.toro.com; www.rainbird.com; www.deere.com.

Do I need to go to college?

The answer to that question depends on your goals. Although a specialized degree from a turf management program is increasingly important, there are still opportunities to advance without one.

For example, a good *turf equipment operator* can move to a *foreman*'s position. With talent, hard work and continuing education with the GCSAA, a foreman may be promoted to the position of assistant superintendent or superintendent.

What are my college options?

Consider two- or four-year programs that lead to associate science/applied science (A.S.) or bachelor of science (B.S.) degrees. Agronomy (soil science) and horticulture (plant science) are common four-year majors. Some colleges offer general turfgrass management majors. Most college programs include general courses in English, history and math.

Technical or professional certificates are one- or two-year programs that do not have a general education component. Instead, they focus exclusively on practical work experience. A good example is the Turf Equipment Technology Certificate offered by Lake City Community College in Lake City, Fla., www.lakecity.cc.fl.us. Penn State University in University Park, Penn., Purdue University in West Lafayette, Ind., and Clemson University in Clemson, S.C., also offer certificate programs.

What if I don't like turf management after a few years?

Indeed, you may tire of working at dawn to ready the course or the pressure of unpredictable weather. The good news is that your experience will make you a valuable employee in other parts of the industry. *Turf equipment manufacturers* (described in the next chapter) welcome salespeople with practical on-course experience. Imagine how convincing you can be selling turf equipment if you can discuss your experience working with it.

CAREERS TO EXPLORE

Career Close-up: GOLF COURSE SUPERINTENDENT

OVERVIEW: Today's *golf course superintendent* has much more to contend with than in decades past. In fact, the position once carried the title of greenkeeper, since greens received most of the attention. Irrigation was not prevalent, so grasses grew according to Mother Nature's plan, and the rough was commonly left in its natural state.

As the design of courses became more sophisticated and the use of irrigation and landscaping more pervasive, the knowledge required by the "greenkeeper" greatly expanded. Accordingly, the name was changed to "superintendent."

DUTIES: An average 18-hole course may have an annual maintenance budget of $258,000, with an additional equipment budget of $55,000 and a payroll of $245,000 (source: GCSAA). The preparation of budgets and long-range turf plans are key responsibilities of the superintendent. Operating within a budget and communicating financial situations to the owner or general manager are essential.

Hiring and managing a staff is also a primary duty. A typical 18-hole golf course will be staffed with an assistant superintendent, foreman, equipment manager and maintenance crew. A course with ornamental flowers and plants may employ a horticulturist (another specialty within turf management). Courses with extensive irrigation systems also may have a permanent irrigation specialist on staff.

SALARY RANGE: In 2000, the median salary for a superintendent in the U.S. was $57,000. Top salaries exceeded $60,000 and entry-level salaries were closer to $35,000. Salaries are higher in the Sun Belt, which has a longer season (source: GCSAA).

JOB OPPORTUNITIES: Although turnover is limited and there are a fixed number of golf courses in the U.S., opportunities are excellent. Superintendents who have worked for a decade or more often turn to careers with less demanding hours. They are sought after as salesmen for turf product companies.

EDUCATION & TRAINING: According to the GCSAA, 96 percent of all superintendents have had some type of formal education beyond high school, with 80 percent having completed at least two years of a formal college program, most with a turf management specialty.

The GCSAA *College Guide* mentioned earlier in the chapter is your best source of information on programs and degrees. The GCSAA Foundation also offers several scholarships.

ENTRY-LEVEL POSITIONS: The career ladder for a superintendent usually requires experience as an assistant superintendent (see below).

GOLF ABILITY & INTEREST: Most superintendents are drawn to their careers because of an interest in golf. It is not necessary to be a par golfer, but a superintendent must know the expectations of highly skilled golfers – they set the maintenance standards at most facilities.

SPECIAL SKILLS & PERSONAL TRAITS: The superintendent must be able to understand a broad range of subjects, from golf course construction to pesticides. Good administrative and executive abilities are required to manage a staff and budget. Most superintendents find that good communication skills are important for dealing with employees and higher-ups. In addition, the position is highly stressful since unpredictable weather and turf diseases can challenge even the most experienced superintendents. This is probably not the position for someone who does not like the pressure of unpredictable situations.

CAREER LADDER & PROMOTION PROSPECTS: Promotions usually involve moving from smaller courses to larger courses, or from public courses to upscale private facilities

ASSISTANT GOLF COURSE SUPERINTENDENT

The *assistant golf course superintendent* reports to the superintendent and may serve as superintendent during the superintendent's absence. At large courses or resorts, there may be more than one assistant superintendent.

The primary duties and educational requirements are similar to those of the superintendent. The median salary in the U.S. in 2000 was $29,000 (source: GCSAA).

The assistant superintendent usually has direct supervision of the maintenance crew, and often chooses the **crew foreman**.

IRRIGATION SPECIALIST

At many facilities, a superintendent with a regular maintenance staff supervises the irrigation system – programming the sprinkler system and making simple repairs. However, large facilities may require a full time **irrigation specialist** – sometimes called an **irrigation technician**.

Many modern-day irrigation systems have sophisticated pumping stations and a computerized network of sprinkler heads. Desert courses can have thousands of sprinkler heads to irrigate ornamental shrubs and plants as well as fairways and greens.

Job opportunities in irrigation are excellent as the number of courses and course renovations increases. As described in Chapter 3, there are several career paths into course irrigation. One of the most important factors, however, is entry-level experience with irrigation systems. Working on the maintenance staff of a golf facility is important because you will learn irrigation systems basics.

With a year of experience on a maintenance crew, you will be eligible for certification programs sponsored by the Irrigation Association, www.irrigation.org. Many irrigation system manufacturers also sponsor training seminars. Two-year certificate programs in turf management also will position you for advanced irrigation work. Lake City Community College in Lake City, Fla., www.lakecity.cc.fl.us, offers a two-year certificate program in irrigation management.

Irrigation specialists often are paid by the hour. The average 1998 hourly wage reported by the GCSAA for irrigation specialists was $9.

EQUIPMENT MANAGER

Every golf course makes a significant investment in the machinery that keeps the fairways, greens and tees in great condition. It is increasingly common for golf facilities to employ an **equipment manager** or **technician** – formerly called a mechanic – to keep machinery in top order.

Today's equipment technician must understand computer systems, including the Global Positioning System found on most machines. He or she must also know how to clean and repair machinery.

The job opportunities in this occupation are among the best in the industry. There are more available positions than qualified applicants, and annual salaries of $75,000 are not unusual. The role of the equipment manager is so essential to the superintendent's success that superintendents often bring their equipment managers along when they change facilities.

The GCSAA identifies the following as top responsibilities of the equipment manager:

> ➤ Inspects, diagnoses and repairs maintenance equipment.
> ➤ Trains maintenance workers in the use of the machines and preventative maintenance.
> ➤ Keeps maintenance records and helps plan the budget for purchases and repairs.

In spite of the heavy demand for trained equipment technicians, programs are hard to find. Lake City Community College in Lake City, Fla., is one of the few colleges that offer a one-year technical certificate program in equipment management. If you have mechanical ability and would like to work with golf machinery, contact your local chapter of the GCSAA and inquire about internships with technicians in your area.

Also look into programs offered by the Equipment & Engine Training Council, www.eetc.org, an organization dedicated to the education of technicians in the outdoor power equipment industry.

INDUSTRY LEADER Q&A

An interview with Scott Woodhead, Golf Operations Manager at Hearst River Golf Course in Dickinson, N.D., and past president of the Golf Course Superintendents Association of America.

Q. **How did you become interested in turf management?**

A. I actually started out studying forestry and then worked in a pro shop for a year. The forestry option wasn't looking so good, so I left school my junior year and went to work on a grounds crew. I was promoted to head greenkeeper after one season and later returned to school.

Q. What's your advice to students who want to get into turf management?

A. Gain experience through summer jobs or internships as you're going through school. Ultimately, a college education is a very important component to this position. In addition to landscape management, agronomy and business management are important to learn.

Q. Where would you direct someone interested in pursuing turf management as a career?

A. I would point them to the GCSAA, which has a career development department as well as student memberships.

Q. How many employees does a superintendent usually manage?

A. It varies depending on the number of holes and the requirements and budget. For an 18-hole facility, 12 to 18 people is normal.

Q. What are their positions?

A. It varies, but typically you have an irrigation technician, a spray technician, a mechanic for all the equipment, one or two assistant superintendents, general grounds keepers and greens keepers, and possibly a horticulturist.

Q. How long is your typical work week?

A. It varies. It's a minimum of 50 hours, but in season, it could easily hit 70 to 75 hours. Then, it's a minimum of 10 hours per day, seven days a week. We don't get holidays off because that's when people like to play golf! And you're always on call because the irrigation system is running at night.

Q. Is it worth the long hours?

A. There have been very few days in the past 25 years that I haven't enjoyed getting up and going to work in the morning. Walking out on the golf course at 5 a.m., when the sun's coming up – there's nothing better. When your office is the great outdoors, what's not to love?

CHAPTER SIX

Careers with Manufacturers

"Try and find a way into the company, and from that position, demonstrate your value and worth to be where you want to be. I call it the Trojan horse strategy."

> Ed Abrain, President,
> Titleist and Cobra – Acushnet Company

In This Chapter:

- How is the golf manufacturing sector divided?
- What occupations exist with manufacturers?
- How do you know if you would be good at sales?
- What are distributors?
- Can I start my own company?
- Learn about the following positions:
     Independent Sales Representative
     Company Sales Representative
     Product Developer
     Management Executive
- Interview with Ed Abrain, President, Titleist and Cobra – Acushnet Company

So far we have learned who manages facilities and who keeps fairways in top condition. But who provides the supplies and machinery needed to do so? And who supplies the products that golfers use to play the game? The answer is manufacturers, our next tour stop.

Who is included among manufacturers?

The manufacturing segment of the golf industry is divided into two main categories: products used by consumers and products used by facilities. The following chart shows a sample of the hundreds of manufactured products.

Consumer Products	Products Used by Facilities	
Balls	Food & Beverage	Ball Washers
Clubs	Fixtures & Furniture	Fertilizers & Chemicals
Apparel	GPS Systems Technology	Golf Cars
Gloves	Point-of-Sale Software	Irrigation Systems
Golf Bags	Tee Time Software	Maintenance Equipment
Tees	Computers	
Other Accessories		

Consumer products are products bought by golfers. Golf balls and clubs are considered hard goods. Accessories, which include clothing, shoes, gloves, tees and golf bags are referred to as soft goods.

The second manufacturing category involves products used by golf facilities. This broad category includes bulldozers, golf cars, ball washers, tee markers, fertilizers, pro shop furniture, snack cars, and even high-tech products such as tee time-reservation software and Global Positioning Systems.

A good way to understand the extent of the manufacturing sector is to visit an industry trade show. Each January, The PGA of America sponsors the PGA Merchandise Show (often referred to as the PGA Expo), in Orlando, Fla.

More than 1,500 manufacturers displayed their products to more than 53,000 industry professionals at the 2001 PGA Expo. Many attendees are buyers selecting merchandise for their golf shops.

In order to attend the show, you have to be an established buyer or seller, but it is possible to attend as a sponsored guest. If you cannot attend, you can see the list of exhibitors (including contact information) on the PGA Expo Web site, www.pgaexpo.com.

The turf industry also has a trade show, sponsored by the Golf Course Superintendents Association of America – usually in February. Sponsored guests also are permitted.

What are the primary careers in manufacturing?

Whether the product is a specialized type of bulldozer for shaping a golf course, a new type of sand wedge, or a new trend in clothing, a ***product designer*** is crucial to the early stages of the manufacturing process. Some products require scientific engineering, while others require graphic design. In new manufacturing companies, the owner may be the product designer.

Integral to product design are marketers who research customer preferences and expectations. Careers in ***marketing*** are covered in Chapter 10 – Careers in Marketing & Public Relations. Another critical function is ***sales*** – more about that later in the chapter.

Manufacturers are headed by ***chief executive officers***, and often need ***financial officers*** or ***treasurers***, along with other managers of critical departments, such as human resources. If a company manufacturers several products, there may even be a ***product manager*** for each.

How is a product brought to market?

After a product is designed and a marketing plan devised, the manufacturing process begins. Usually the designer will submit a set of specifications to a manufacturer. Perhaps it is a foundry for club components, or a pattern-maker for a clothing manufacturer. (Except for a handful of products, the factory employees who manufacture golf products do not have to know much about the game. For that reason, jobs such as factory worker and plant manager are not included in this book.)

One of the most critical challenges for a manufacturer is to develop the right sales staff because, after all, the primary interest of the manufacturer is to sell its products. This chapter explains in detail the types of sales positions available in the manufacturing sector.

How do I decide where to work in manufacturing?

With thousands of companies and dozens of job positions in golf manufacturing, it can be overwhelming deciding where to look. A good approach is to consider what you like to talk about, where you like to work and what your skills are.

Are you mechanical and interested in the horsepower of an engine, or would you rather talk about the fabric of a golf shirt? Do you prefer to work with golf clubs or golf cars? Is designing Internet software your passion? Or are you an engineer who prefers to analyze designs in the quiet of an office? Do you like big corporate organizations or small entrepreneurial ones? Answering these questions will not only help you decide what type of manufacturer you would like to work for, but the appropriate positions as well.

The choices may be easier to make when you understand more about the distribution and sale of products.

What are turf product distributors?

In the turf side of the industry, manufacturers seldom sell directly to the end customer. Customers such as golf course superintendents do not want to choose a $50,000 machine from a catalog. The superintendent wants to see the machine in a show room, look under the hood and be able to rely on a local service department for repairs.

For those reasons, manufacturers of turf equipment and products often sell products to a ***distributor*** or ***dealer*** who resells them to the final customer and provides repair services. The distributor usually maintains a regional showroom with a staff of salespeople who build relationships with the courses in their area.

The good news to someone looking for a career selling turf products is that there are two levels of sales opportunities. The first is selling from the manufacturer to the distributor/dealer, and the second is selling from the distributor/dealer to the final customer.

How are consumer products distributed?

In the consumer segment, manufacturers generally sell directly to retail channels, which then sell to golfers.

The National Golf Foundation categorizes retail channels as follows:
- ➢ Mass merchant
- ➢ On-course retailer
- ➢ Off-course retailer
- ➢ Sporting goods store
- ➢ Warehouse club
- ➢ Mail order
- ➢ Custom club maker
- ➢ Other, including Internet

(The next chapter in this book explores the retail sales channels in more detail.)

What are the opportunities in high-tech products and software?

Almost every golf facility now uses some type of software – for tee time reservations, dining room scheduling or to run a Web site. Manufacturers of golf-specific software often have exhibits at the major trade shows.

If you would like to work at a golf software company, search the golf employment Web sites. There may not be a "software" or "technology" job category so the best bet is to search for employers in the software business. At www.golfingcareers.com you also can search for positions using key technology terms, such as "Web," "interactive" or "software."

What is a "sales rep?"

Whether working for a manufacturer of golf bags or fertilizers, a *salesperson* is often called a *sales rep*. This is short for "representative" of the manufacturer. (Remember that salespeople with a manufacturer are different from salespeople in a golf shop or other retail outlet. Positions in retail sales are covered in the next chapter.)

What are the different types of sales reps?

Sales representatives employed by a manufacturer are called *company reps*, *inside reps* or *direct reps*. As company employees they receive benefits such as health insurance and retirement plans and are generally reimbursed for travel and entertainment expenses.

The *independent sales rep* – sometimes called a *manufacturer's rep* – is an independent contractor who receives no corporate benefits and pays all of his or her expenses.

Why do manufacturers use different types of sales reps?

Fundamental to understanding sales positions in the golf industry is to understand that commissions comprise a majority of most salespeople's incomes. The more products sold, the bigger the commissions.

Large manufacturers sell enough products to maintain a permanent sales staff. Here's how it works. A large manufacturer assigns a geographic territory or region to a single employee. If the region is large and the product is popular, a good salesperson will earn enough commission selling one manufacturer's products. The manufacturer benefits from employing a staff that focuses only on its product line.

On the other hand, a small manufacturer or a start-up may sell its products only in a small region – or only in small quantities.

For example, let's say that a designer created a fancy and expensive line of golf club covers. Only a few shops might be interested in carrying them. Under those circumstances, a salesperson would not be able to earn enough commission selling only those club covers.

The solution is for the independent rep to carry several different products and hope to sell enough of each to earn adequate commissions. The independent sales rep might carry club covers, golf towels, shoe bags and fancy hats. As long as the products do not compete, an independent sales rep can carry dozens of products and show them to many customers in a geographic region.

There are many manufacturers who use independent sales reps, and many sales reps who make an excellent salary this way.

How do you know if you would be good at sales?

Dawn Schlesinger is president of Golfsurfin.com, an Internet employment site specializing in the golf industry, www.golfsurfin.com. Prior to her work at Golfsurfin, Dawn founded a recruiting firm specializing in sales positions. Dawn offers the following advice to help you determine if you would be good at sales:

"There are five key factors you must consider when evaluating your personality to see if you would be a successful salesperson.

1. *Discipline*: Most sales positions have daily, monthly or quarterly quotas. In order to meet quotas, a good salesperson must be disciplined enough to make new contacts daily. Good salespeople must be creative and disciplined enough to drum up business and uncover new prospects. A career in sales does not offer significant structure and guidance.

2. *Competitiveness*: Do you love the satisfaction you get from winning? Almost all sales jobs involve convincing someone that your product or service is the right solution, even when the customer thinks it is not. If you are persuasive, you will be able to turn a "no" into a "yes." All great sales people truly enjoy winning their argument.

3. *Presentation skills*: Good salespeople are articulate and able to present

products or services concisely. People who have a tough time getting to the point, or who are too technically minded to explain things clearly, will not fare well.

4. *Listening skills:* This is probably the greatest asset a good salesperson can have. If you can get people to talk about their problems and goals, you will be successful in sales. People who like to hear themselves talk or who try to sell products and services that are irrelevant to the customer do not last long.

5. *Handling rejection:* This seems to be the most difficult aspect of selling. No one likes to be rejected, but it is part of the job and should not be taken personally. Good salespeople psyche themselves up with thoughts like, "The word 'no' is to be viewed as a challenge." I think each successful salesperson has his or her own way of dealing with rejection – with a little creativity and positive thinking it will not stop them from closing a deal.

A few additional points:

Are you motivated by money? Do you like to be recognized among your peers? Would you enjoy rapid career growth into sales management? If you are the type of person that enjoys such rewards, sales may be the career for you.

Look for sales positions that fit your style: People who need constant gratification would be better suited to "activity driven" sales positions, such as calling on many accounts each week, and a person who possesses solid relationship-building skills would fare better working on one account over longer periods of time.

Finally, it is imperative that a salesperson believes in the product or service they chose to sell."

Can I move into golf sales from a different industry?

If you have had a successful sales career in an another industry and you love golf, it is possible to move into the golf industry. The large manufacturers who hire permanent sales staff generally require three to five years of sales experience and golf knowledge.

How do I find sales positions with manufacturers?

Of all the occupations in the golf industry, sales positions are probably the easiest to find.

If you think you would like to work for a manufacturer, visit employment or manufacturers' Web sites. Here are some familiar names of manufacturers that produce products for consumers. Many manufacturers sites have "About us" sections or may even have employment opportunities listed on their sites. If there is a specific manufacturer you are looking for and you do not have their Web address, try using a search engine like www.google.com.

➢ Ashworth: www.ashworthinc.com
➢ Belding: www.beldingsports.com
➢ Burton: www.burtongolf.com
➢ Callaway: www.callawaygolf.com
➢ Cutter & Buck: www.cutterandbuck.com
➢ FootJoy: www.footjoy.com
➢ Izod: www.izod.com
➢ Maxfli: www.maxfli.com
➢ Mizuno: www.mizuno.com
➢ Nike Golf: www.nikegolf.com
➢ Ping: www.pinggolf.com
➢ Reebok: www.reebok.com
➢ Spalding: www.spalding.com
➢ Taylor Made: www.taylormadegolf.com
➢ Titleist: www.titleist.com
➢ Wilson: www.wilsonsports.com

If the idea of being an independent sales representative appeals to you, you also will find employment Web sites helpful. In addition, contact the National Golf Sales Representatives Association, which serves independent sales reps (480-860-6348).

Also don't forget to check the classified section of your newspaper for general sales positions. Most will not be in the golf industry, but you could get lucky.

Can I start my own manufacturing business?

Of course. Every year hundreds of new golf products hit the market. Generally, the road an entrepreneur travels is rough, but high risk sometimes means high rewards.

Expect to contract with designers who can write up detailed specifications of your product. Engineering help also may be needed.

If you have a product idea, the first step is to find investors – preferably with experience. Potential investors will want to see a business plan that projects costs and revenues. *How to Write a Great Business Plan*, an article by William A. Sahlman, is available from Harvard Business School Publications (reprint #97409; www.hbsp.harvard.edu; 617-783-7410). Also, see www.sportbuddy.com for a good example of a golf start-up. Melissa Montague started Sport Buddy, a golf hat company, in 1999.

CAREERS TO EXPLORE

Career Close-up: INDEPENDENT SALES REPRESENTATIVE

OVERVIEW: The *independent sales rep* is self-employed and pays his or her expenses for travel, meals, entertainment, office rental and assistants' salaries. Most independent sales reps form small self-owned corporations.

Independent sales reps have no clock to punch, so they must be self-starters and self-educators. If you expect formal training and handholding, this is not the career for you.

DUTIES: A primary duty is to learn everything about the products you are representing so that you can best present them to customers.

If a rep is not given an established contact list, he or she must find a way to identify buyers. This is not like working in a retail store, where customers walk in the door. In interviews, it is a good idea to ask whether a manufacturer provides leads or expects you to find them yourself.

Selling a product often requires more than just showing the buyer how it works. The sales representative may have to advise the customer on how to merchandise the product, how to project demand and whether to buy the product on a seasonal basis. A salesperson should receive training from a manufacturer to help the buyer make these decisions.

The most important duty, however, is to make the sale. Hundreds of books have been written about how to be a good salesperson. Yet successful salespeople seem to come by the skill naturally. Many learned they had sales skills early in life, such as during a high school job.

A final responsibility is to make sure the customer is satisfied. That means contacting the buyer after the sale. Many successful salespeople consider the after-sale call crucial to establishing a good customer relationship.

SALARY RANGE: Entry-level salaries start at $20,000 annually, but salaries increase as salespeople build a customer base. The average annual salary after expenses is $45,000. Very high producers can make more than $100,000 a year.

JOB OPPORTUNITIES: Intelligent, responsible sales representatives are in demand, so opportunities are good to excellent.

EDUCATION & TRAINING: A college degree – with a major in business or marketing – is helpful, but not essential. On-the-job train-

---

JOB HUNTING TIPS:

Attend trade shows to see "job boards"

The PGA Merchandise Show has several "job boards" where companies post independent sales representatives positions. Look for the booth of the National Golf Sales Representatives Association, which has one of the largest job boards. The Golf Course Superintendents Association of America trade show www.gcsaa.org, also has an electronic job-posting board. Don't forget to use the employment Web sites. They are a great way to learn about the types of positions available.

ing remains the best education. Some manufacturers prefer to hire representatives who have worked as golf professionals.

ENTRY-LEVEL POSITIONS: Look for any position that provides sales experience – even if outside the golf industry. Experience as a buyer is also recommended. With sales experience on your résumé, it will be easier to land a job in golf and advance up the ranks.

GOLF ABILITY & INTEREST: An understanding of golf is essential whether you are selling clubs, balls or soft goods. Most sales reps of high-end golf equipment are good golfers. On the turf equipment and maintenance side, course experience is helpful and turf management knowledge is essential.

SPECIAL SKILLS & PERSONAL TRAITS: The independent sales rep has to be self-motivated and entrepreneurial. Long-term success depends on the salesperson's integrity and reliability, and the ability to develop relationships with customers.

CAREER LADDER & PROMOTION PROSPECTS: Experienced sales representatives move up by looking for positions in better territories – those with more customers and greater opportunity for commissions. Salespeople also can advance into positions as *regional or national sales managers* for manufacturers.

COMPANY SALES REPRESENTATIVE

Positions as a *company representative* are more limited than those for independent representatives. Manufacturers are more selective and require several years of selling experience, sometimes in a specific segment of the industry. Manufacturers do, however, offer more training. They will hire a salesperson with a good track record from another manufacturer and then provide training in their own products. A company rep has more administrative responsibilities and may have to compile sales reports.

The company rep is not his or her own boss; he or she trades the freedom of the independent rep for the security and benefits offered by a large corporation. Many successful company reps eventually move into management positions – perhaps as regional or national sales managers.

PRODUCT DEVELOPMENT – GOLF CLUB EQUIPMENT

Most golfers do not appreciate the extensive research that goes into creating golf equipment. Most major golf club and ball manufacturers employ a team of engineers to work on *product development and design*. These are not just ordinary engineers – they are engineers who like golf and understand the game.

SOUND BITES FROM INDEPENDENT SALES REPS

Positive

"There's lots of freedom."

"You meet people from all walks of life. New opportunities are always arising."

Negative

"The industry lags behind in sales technology."

"You have to return every call from a customer – even when you're on vacation."

"If you can't sell, you become unemployed."

JOB HUNTING TIPS:

Don't forget the turf sector

Don't overlook sales positions in the turf sector. It is easy to glamorize consumer products because they are so visible in magazines and on television. But the turf sector is just as important to the golf industry and just as lucrative to salespeople. This could be the path for you, especially if you are technically minded.

The principal duties of a product designer are to design, develop and test golf equipment. Most equipment designers work for golf manufacturers. The senior position within a product development department is usually the vice president.

Some companies specialize in specific types of clubs, such as putters. Others, like Golfsmith, design all types of clubs for their own brand, as well as custom-made clubs for other manufacturers. The Golfsmith Web site, www.golfsmith.com, is a good place to begin your education in product development.

Annual salaries for a starting engineer with a B.S. degree range from $35,000 to $45,000. Engineers with experience earn closer to $50,000, and annual salaries of the top engineers can reach $200,000.

Job opportunities are very competitive because the profession is small. It helps to have had experience in club repair and club making prior to your formal education.

A college degree is suggested and a B.S. degree in mechanical engineering, physics or metallurgy is recommended. Some designers have worked previously in the aerospace industry. Although it is possible to enter the field after years as a hobbyist designing you own clubs, an engineering degree is key for advancement within larger companies.

Golf skills are critical. Although many designers complain that the demanding nature of their work keeps them from playing, most are still very good golfers. They have to be to do what they do.

> **SOUND BITES FROM PRODUCT DESIGNERS**
>
> "Where else can you have clubs in your office and putt during the day without your boss looking at you funny?"
>
> "Very challenging; lots of fun."
>
> "It is satisfying to have people thank you for making something that brings them pleasure and enjoyment."

MANAGEMENT EXECUTIVE IN MANUFACTURING COMPANY

It is very easy to be the **president or CEO** of a manufacturing company – if you start your own company. It is much harder to work your way through the ranks.

In a new company, the founder may serve as **chief executive officer** and **chief operating officer** for a very small staff. As the company grows, the founder will hire other executives to manage key functions like manufacturing, marketing, sales, product development, human resources, finance and legal affairs.

At the head of each of these departments is a **vice president** or **director**. The larger the company, the more employees each vice president oversees. A small start up may have a dozen employees, while industry leaders like Callaway and Titleist employ thousands.

There is nothing wrong with aiming for a position as president of a successful golf manufacturing company, so long as the challenge and difficulty are recognized. It may be more practical to aspire to other management positions.

Most executives in established companies have been promoted to their positions. A common pattern is to enter as salesperson and then be promoted to regional or national sales manager. But entry-level positions in marketing and finance offer promotion opportunities as well. The larger and well-established golf manufacturers, such as Nike and Callaway, seek employees with four or five years of experience for management positions. Some good advice from the executives we surveyed is to work for a small company first and learn how to manage a staff.

When it comes to golf ability and interest, most executives say that it is more important to understand the culture of golf than to be an excellent player.

INDUSTRY LEADER Q&A

An interview with Ed Abrain, President, Titleist and Cobra–Acushnet Company, located in Fairhaven, Mass.

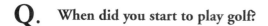

Q. **When did you start to play golf?**

A. I had played as a kid, but not avidly. I was a baseball, hockey and football player. I didn't really start playing until I was about 20 years old.

Q. **How did you get into the manufacturing side of golf?**

A. Acushnet had just purchased Golf Craft in Escondido, California. They were looking for someone with business diversity – operations knowledge, a formal financial background, and an understanding of manufacturing systems and management planning systems. I went to California to get the plant to adopt the Titleist culture. When I returned in 1972, I was brought into international business. In the '70s, the U.S. was where the bulk of the business was. I was asked to become the international business manager for Titleist and to go examine our international contacts and come back with a plan. I spent the first three to five months trying to find out about golf in the international world.

Q. What should someone's strategy be for breaking into the golf business?

A. They should do the research necessary to identify and understand the segments of the industry that appeal to them – marketing, retail, sports management, facility management, architecture, etc. There are so many segments; they need to think about all of them and match their own skills and ambitions. They also need to examine which of the industry segments are showing the highest growth.

Q. What advice would you give to someone who wants to work for a large golf product manufacturer?

A. You have to establish realistic expectations. A lot of guys with business degrees immediately want to be executives, but may end up in the customer service department. Initially that's challenging to their self-esteem, but by starting in that area and learning the product, that's where we take our sales and marketing trainees from.

Q. Besides understanding their product lines, what should you know about a manufacturer before interviewing with them?

A. You ought to understand the company's philosophy.

Q. What training programs are available at Acushnet?

A. We have formalized training by department. It's not merely academic in nature, it's on-the-job training. For future marketing and salespeople, we have a technical rep program in our customer service department. If a customer has a specific question about the 990 B clubs, they'll go to a tech rep. The next step is for the person to work in field training or a start-up position in the marketing department. There are similar programs in R&D (research & development) and manufacturing.

CHAPTER SEVEN

Careers in Retail

"To get a position in golf retail, it helps to have experience – not necessarily in golf, but in a summer retail job or other customer service position."

Maggie Arendt, President,
Association of Golf Merchandisers

In This Chapter:

- What does the retail sector include?
- What positions exist in retail?
- What are the different retail channels?
- Do I have to be a golf professional?
- What is the Association of Golf Merchandisers?
- Learn about the following positions:
  Merchandise Buyer
  Store Manager
  Sales Associate
- Interview with Maggie Arendt, President, Association of Golf Merchandisers

Where did you buy your golf clubs, putter, favorite golf shirt or those special solid-core golf balls? Whatever your answer, you named a golf retail channel. "Retail" is a trade term used to identify where consumers – golfers like you and me – purchase their equipment, clothing and other supplies.

The National Golf Foundation reported that in 1999 consumers spent more than $4.2 billion on balls, clubs and accessories such as gloves, bags, tees and towels. That number is about 25 percent of the total consumer spending on golf, which includes green fees. To dispel any myths that this is just a man's game, the average female golfer spent about $411 on golf annually in 1999, while the average male spent $462.

Industry observers pay close attention to consumer spending because it is a barometer of interest in the game. An increase in spending on golf clubs indicates that people are investing in the game for the long term. This translates to more golfers and more rounds played, which encourages developers to build more courses and manufacturers to produce more goods. Of course, a decrease in consumer spending signals a less optimistic outlook.

What positions are available in retail?

Every retail shop or store that sells golf products has three distinct functions – and three distinct occupations: buying the merchandise, managing the store and selling the merchandise to customers. In a very small golf shop, a single person might have all three duties: ***merchandise buyer***, ***store manager*** and ***sales associate***. But, most likely, the jobs are performed by three or more separate people.

Before we can tour those careers, it will be helpful to understand the different types of retail operations. Occupations with the same title differ significantly depending on the retail outlet. For example, the store manager of a large resort pro shop has duties different from the manager of the golf department in a Wal-Mart.

What are the different retail sale channels?

The National Golf Foundation categorizes retail businesses by eight channels of distribution: (These were mentioned briefly in the last chapter, but are explained in more detail here.)

JOB HUNTING TIPS:

Learn from the ground up

Working as a sales clerk in a retail golf shop is an excellent entry-level position. When reviewing opportunities in the golf retail segment, always make sure you understand the channel you will be working in.

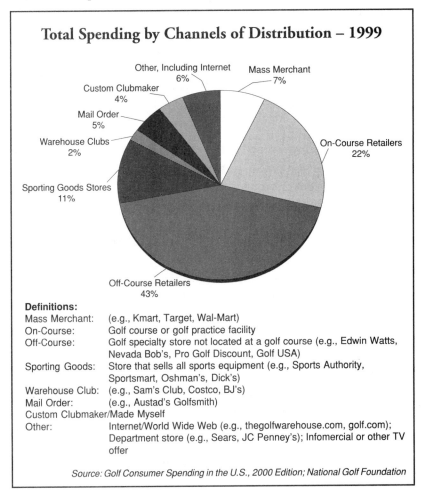

Total Spending by Channels of Distribution – 1999

- Other, Including Internet 6%
- Mass Merchant 7%
- Custom Clubmaker 4%
- Mail Order 5%
- Warehouse Clubs 2%
- Sporting Goods Stores 11%
- On-Course Retailers 22%
- Off-Course Retailers 43%

Definitions:

Mass Merchant:	(e.g., Kmart, Target, Wal-Mart)
On-Course:	Golf course or golf practice facility
Off-Course:	Golf specialty store not located at a golf course (e.g., Edwin Watts, Nevada Bob's, Pro Golf Discount, Golf USA)
Sporting Goods:	Store that sells all sports equipment (e.g., Sports Authority, Sportsmart, Oshman's, Dick's)
Warehouse Club:	(e.g., Sam's Club, Costco, BJ's)
Mail Order:	(e.g., Austad's Golfsmith)
Custom Clubmaker/Made Myself	
Other:	Internet/World Wide Web (e.g., thegolfwarehouse.com, golf.com); Department store (e.g., Sears, JC Penney's); Infomercial or other TV offer

Source: Golf Consumer Spending in the U.S., 2000 Edition; National Golf Foundation

What are "on-course" retailers?

Shops at golf courses are referred to as "on-course" retailers. It is not surprising that on-course retailers are the largest category of retail operations – with more than 15,000 shops – a little less than the number of courses in the country. Sometimes the term "green grass shop" is used to distinguish on-course shops from golf stores in commercial shopping areas – sometimes called "cement shops."

How are on-course operations managed?

There are two types of management at on-course shops.

The most common is when the *head professional* or *director of golf* (described in Chapter 8) manages retail operations. Profit from the operations supplements his or her salary from the facility. The head pro usually hires the staff and bears the salary expense, buys the merchandise (or hires a buyer), provides lessons (or hires instructors), and, in some shops, even invests in shop décor. The good news is that if the merchandise sells well and customers are satisfied, the head golf pro can make a nice profit.

At other courses, especially large resorts or facilities managed by a golf management company, the facility retains ownership of the retail operations and profits. The facility hires a *store manager* and *merchandise buyer* along with a head professional for managing tee times and other golf-specific operations, such as instruction.

A significant difference between the retail operations of small and large facilities is in the area of market research. At a small club with a few hundred members, the golf professional usually has a good understanding of his customers' preferences. At a large resort, however, the customer base is diverse, and market research may be needed to identify customer preferences. This is where a background in marketing is very helpful.

Do I have to be a golf professional to work at an on-course pro shop?

The bad news is that it may be difficult to find an entry-level position in an on-course shop unless you are an apprentice in a golf professional program, such as those run by The PGA of America or LPGA.

Many head professionals are graduates of these programs and prefer to hire assistants with the same background. In addition, many shop assistant positions are filled by word-of-mouth or the members-only "job boards" of The PGA of America's and LPGA's professional schools.

The good news is that if you are not interested in becoming a golf professional but would like to work in retail, you still have options. For example, shops at larger resorts and those operated by golf-management companies often hire buyers and managers with retail experience, rather than people aspiring to be golf professionals.

What about off-course retailers?

Although the category of on-course retailers comprises the largest number of shops, off-course retailers brought in the most revenue in 1999. Off-course shops are devoted exclusively to golf, but are not located on a course. Nearly 50 percent of the revenue at off-course retailers comes from golf club sales.

Some off-course retailers are national operations, but most are privately owned shops with one or two locations. Following are two examples of national off-course retailers:

> ➤ Edwin Watts Golf Shops: www.edwinwatts.com.
> ➤ The PGA Tour Shops

Although it is a plus to have completed a PGA of America or LPGA certificate program to work for off-course retailers, it is not essential to entry-level positions, so long as you are a good golfer and can build on your experience.

What are some other retail channels?

While two-thirds of all consumer spending occurs in on-course and off-course shops, the remaining third are made by consumers at several other types of retail operations, which are explained below.

Sporting goods stores sell only sports equipment. Some are national chains – The Sports Authority, for example. But there are also several large regional sports stores such as Oshmann's or Dick's.

Mass merchants such as Kmart, Target, and Wal-Mart, and warehouse clubs such as Costco and Sam's Club, also sell golf equipment. (Web sites are www.bluelight.com for Kmart, www.target.com for Target, www.walmart.com for Wal-Mart, www.costco.com for Costco and www.samsclub.com for Sam's Club.) Entry-level positions with any of these large retailers, which offer training programs, will provide critical experience in buying, sales and management. Although you may not be able to specialize in golf products, working for these large retailers may position you for a move into golf specialty retailers.

The mail order business is another sales channel with career opportunities. Although most mail order retailers do not have bricks and mortar shops, they still require buyers and managers.

> ➤ Golfsmith is one of largest and oldest golf mail order business: www.golfsmith.com
> ➤ The Women's Golf Company, founded by Mary Ellen Hart, a former sporting goods executive is a younger operation: www.womensgolf.com

---

JOB HUNTING TIPS:

Take a marketing seminar to learn about retailing

Although you may choose a career in the golf industry because you like to play the game, your income potential may depend more on your ability to manage retail operations. Player Instruction colleges and programs are continually upgrading classes in merchandising and retailing. Other associations, such as the Association of Golf Merchandisers, www.agmgolf.org, offer marketing seminars to round out the retail skills of the golf professional.

As the competition increases for pro shop jobs, applicants and employees are likely to receive increased scrutiny. Directors of golf will be paying more attention to the business skills of their assistants. The ability to teach will always be important, but customer service skills will be increasingly valuable.

What about custom club fitting?

Another retail outlet is the "build it yourself" channel. Since clubs are manufactured from component parts – club head, shaft and grip – it has always been possible to specialize in *custom club making*. Tour players usually have their clubs built to match their swing characteristics and body types – especially when endorsements from club manufacturers are involved.

Over the past several decades it has become easier to obtain component parts and build clubs, either as a hobby or as an occupation. Some large golf club manufacturers are beginning to offer custom fitting, so experience as a club maker may position you for careers with manufacturers.

Club repair also is related to this field. Many large golf shops offer club repair services. The shops may employ on-site or off-site repair professionals. An occupation in club repair often leads to a career as a custom club maker.

Many club repair and fitting businesses are small and entrepreneurial. One of the benefits of working for one is being able to manage your own schedule and find time for a round of golf.

Following are three companies that offer classes in club making, repair and fitting. Generally, week-long programs cost around $350.

➤ Dynacraft: www.dynacraftgolf.com; 800-321-4833
➤ Golfsmith International: www.golfsmith.com; 800-456-3344
➤ GolfWorks: www.golfworks.com; 800-848-8358

The Professional Clubmakers' Society, www.proclubmakers.org, was founded in 1989 to promote and elevate the profession of club fitting, building and repair. PCS, which has more than 1,300 members, developed a certification program and sponsors several seminars throughout the year.

What about careers with Internet retailers?

Several years ago it looked like the Internet would revolutionize the golf retail industry, with many Web sites flourishing, but the category has lost some momentum.

Much of the software used by online golf retailers does not require specific knowledge of golf. If you would like to work for one of these companies, you can locate them using a search engine (use the key words: "golf club" and "purchase" and hundreds will pop up). Most Web sites make it easy to inquire about jobs. If you do not see an "employment" or "job opportunity" tab, go to the corporate or "about us" section. If that is not available, check the bottom of the home page, where you may find another link or the name of the Web master.

JOB HUNTING TIPS:

Use the Web to find off-course retail jobs

Some regional retailers post job opportunities on their Web sites. If you don't know the names of local retailers, use www.yellowpages.com to search for "golf shops." The Yellow Pages provide only address and telephone numbers – not Web sites.

Since off-course retailers don't have captive customers like on-course shops, they must pay more attention to merchandising, marketing and customer service. Accordingly, they will hire people with specific marketing, business development and retail skills – sometimes from outside the golf industry. This is a good way for mid-career professionals to move into the golf industry.

What is the difference between a sales position in a retail store and being a sales rep?

In Chapter 6, the position of *sales rep* was discussed, along with some thoughts on how to know if you would be good at sales. There are certainly general skills that apply to all sales jobs, including working behind the counter at a pro shop. Knowing how to provide good customer service is an example.

But retail sales positions do not involve finding the customer or making cold calls. In retail, the customer has already walked through your door. Your job is to help the customer make a selection – often with personal considerations in mind. The customer may ask, "Will I like this putter?" "Does this shirt look good on me?" If you don't like this kind of personal interaction, you may prefer being a sales rep and answering, "Will my customers like this shirt?"

Where can I learn more about merchandising?

Merchandising – sometimes refereed to as retailing – has become a more specialized profession due to the efforts of the Association of Golf Merchandisers, www.agmgolf.org. The AGM has 800 members (including buyers and suppliers) and offers a special membership to college students. The AGM sponsors seminars and publishes a merchandise manual that contains step-by-step instructions on planning inventory and sales. Publication information is available on the AGM Web site, which also posts job openings in retail operations.

CAREERS TO EXPLORE

Career Close-up: MERCHANDISE BUYER

OVERVIEW: The *merchandise buyer* is a key position in any retail operation. In some on-course operations, the golf professional is the buyer. This section, however, focuses on merchandise buying as a specialized career. When a buyer has responsibility for several shops, the title *director of retail* may be used.

Many large retail operations (including mass merchants and specialty sports stores) hire or consult with experienced merchandise buyers. Consider that at a busy resort, more than 100,000 customers a year may walk through the golf shop to sign in for tee times. If the merchandise appeals to customers, the revenue from the shop will be an important part of the facility's profits. The shop's owner will make a good investment hiring an experienced merchandise buyer.

Merchandise buying in the golf industry is challenging because consumers are so diverse. On any given day, a shop's customers will range from expert to beginning golfers. Some will be affluent or fashion conscious. Others will be interested mostly in economic value.

DUTIES: The principal duty of the merchandise buyer is to stock products that customers will want to buy. The task sounds easy, but, of course, it is not. There are thousands of items from which to choose, and the choices are overwhelming to those without training. Buyers have an opportunity to look at merchandise at industry trade shows, such as the PGA Merchandise Show.

Some buyers specialize in different products. At a very large specialty store, there may be separate buyers for clubs, clothes and even shoes.

SALARY RANGE: The starting salary of an *assistant buyer* is about $22,000. Experienced buyers can be paid up to $80,000 a year.

JOB OPPORTUNITIES: Opportunities are excellent as more facilities look to streamline retail operations and increase revenue. This is a fast-track career once you establish a good reputation.

EDUCATION & TRAINING: Although some buyers have risen from sales positions, a more formal route is to obtain a college degree in marketing or business. College should be followed by several years of experience with a large retailer. Learning how to develop a buying plan is very helpful. Computer literacy is increasingly important for spreadsheet analysis and communication with suppliers.

ENTRY-LEVEL POSITIONS: One of the best entry-level positions is to work as a *shop assistant* for a retailer with an experienced buyer who might serve as a mentor. Work as an assistant can be menial; you might find yourself folding merchandise and keeping displays neat.

GOLF ABILITY & INTEREST: An understanding of golf is essential if you are selling clubs and other equipment. It is less important if you are selling clothing.

SPECIAL SKILLS: On the clothing and accessory side, it helps to have a flair for fashion. As one buyer put it: "You have to like to shop."

STORE MANAGER

Some of the largest golf specialty stores are bigger than 30,000 square feet. That's more stock to manage, more cash registers to monitor and more employees to oversee. As the size of many off-course retailers grows, the need for talented *store managers* also grows.

There is no formal career path to becoming a store manager. If you have good communication skills and experience in store management, you may want to consider becoming a store manager for a golf retailer.

A typical entry-level position is that of *sales associate*. Once you have shown that you are dependable and tenacious, look for opportunities to take on more responsibility. Another route is to move into golf after experience as a store manager in another area.

Store manager positions are occasionally posted on employment Web sites, but it may be more effective to directly contact golf retail stores in your area.

SALES ASSISTANT

The advice we heard time and again is to simply "get a foot in the door." Take any job you can in sales. You will not find "golf retail sales" positions in most newspaper classified ads, but they frequently are posted on employment Web sites. When searching, make sure you include the word "retail" to avoid turning up manufacturers' sales representative positions.

INDUSTRY LEADER Q&A

An interview with Maggie Arendt, the Executive Director of the Association of Golf Merchandisers, a non-profit association of golf retail buyers and suppliers located in Fountain Hills, Ariz.

Q. **What type of experience is necessary to work in golf retailing?**

A. It helps to have customer service or retail experience – not necessarily in golf. Even a summer job in an apparel specialty store is a start.

Q. **What's the best way to determine if you want to work in this field?**

A. Go to a golf shop and ask to talk to a golf pro or buyer about golf retailing. The AGM also has two national conferences a year the day before the PGA Merchandise Shows in Las Vegas and Orlando. We welcome anyone. Retailers from all over the country attend—from beginners to seasoned professionals. We also hold regional seminars.

Q. What's changed in the past several years in golf retail?

A. Both the selection of merchandise and the personnel have changed. Club-fitting systems have put sales of hard goods back into green-grass stores, and most larger facilities now have directors of retail to choose from the incredible variety of merchandise available. Also, more women with mainstream retail experience are being hired as managers or buyers for golf shops.

Q. How do the roles of golf pro and buyer differ?

A. Golf pros generally focus on purchasing hard goods, in addition to teaching, conducting tournaments and setting up tee times. Buyers focus on selecting soft goods, hiring retail staff, and merchandise presentation and sales.

CHAPTER EIGHT

Careers in Player Instruction – The Golf Professional

"You have to have a love, and great empathy, for people. You have to care more about others than yourself. If you're a great player and always worried about your own game, you probably are not going to be a great teacher. Great teachers are also life-long learners."

Gary Wiren, Founder of the PGA National
Academy of Golf, currently Chairman of
Golf Around the World, Inc.

In This Chapter:

- What does it mean to be a golf professional?
- How good a golfer do I have to be?
- What are the roles of The PGA of America and the LPGA Teaching and Club Professional Division?
- What about career colleges for golf instruction?
- How do I become a Tour pro?
- Learn about the following positions:
  - Director of Golf
  - Head Golf Professional
  - Director of Instruction
- Interview with Gary Wiren, Chairman and Founder, Golf Around the World, Inc.

Ask any serious junior golfer what he or she wants to be, and "golf pro" probably ranks just behind "tour player." In fact, some readers were probably disappointed that our career tour did not begin with this chapter. But with the previous seven chapter stops behind us, we are now ready to learn about one of the most popular careers in the golf industry.

One of the first steps in understanding what is required to be a golf pro is knowing that anyone can call themselves a golf pro, golf teacher or golf instructor. However, there are certifications and accredited courses of study, which you will learn about later in this chapter, that lend legitimacy to the title.

What is a golf professional?

Hopefully, a short historical detour will help answer that question.

The PGA of America, founded in 1916, and the Ladies Professional Golf Association (LPGA), founded in 1950, adopted the word "professional" in the names of their organizations to convey the fact that the game was more than a hobby – it was a line of work, a profession.

The short term "pro" came into use and the members of the associations became known as either "touring pros" or "club pros." Touring pros traveled around the country conducting exhibitions and playing tournaments. Among the early touring pros were Walter Hagen and Babe Zaharias.

The club pro, on the other hand, was usually an employee of a golf club who played golf with members, gave a few lessons and maintained a small shop where clubs and balls were sold.

In the '60s, television coverage of golf brought the game into the living rooms of millions of Americans. The next step was for those Americans to take to the fairways. As more people took up the game, club professionals began offering more golf instruction, and the title *golf teacher* or *golf instructor* became more popular. (The terms "instructor" and "teacher" are used interchangeably in this chapter.)

Recognizing the importance of teaching as a career, the LPGA established a special teacher-training division within its association in 1959. Instruction became an increasingly important skill for golf professionals certified by The PGA of America, as well.

Today, the term *golf professional* generally implies a person qualified to teach the game as well as manage a golf facility. The term "golf instructor" suggests a stronger focus on teaching than on management. The PGA of America has more than 25 different classifications for its "professionals."

How good a golfer do I have to be to be a professional?

You must be a very good golfer to become a certified golf professional.

The PGA of America and the LPGA Teaching and Club Professional Division have established a benchmark for certification through a Playing Ability Test – often referred to as the "PAT." The good news is that you only have to pass it once.

The PGA of America PAT requires students to score within 15 shots of the course rating for 36 consecutive holes to qualify for final certification and membership. Generally that requires about an 8 handicap. To qualify for admission to the LPGA program, women must shoot 85 or lower on a course of 5,700 to 5,900 yards.

Other golf instruction schools discussed below have playing ability requirements – although they are not quite as tough as The PGA of America and LPGA PATs.

How do I become a golf instructor?

The two oldest, most prestigious, and best-known golf instructor programs are those offered by The PGA of America and the LPGA Teaching and Club Professional Division (LPGA T&CP). Although The PGA of America and LPGA programs prepare students to work in many different sectors of the golf industry, including management, and marketing and sales, a majority of students enter the programs with a teaching career in mind.

After passing the Playing Ability Test described above, completing required classes and seminars, and apprenticing in a golf facility, students become members of The PGA of America or LPGA T&CP division. There are more than 26,000 PGA members and more than 1,200 LPGA T&CP members. Many golf professionals include "PGA Member" or "LPGA Member" on their business cards.

How do I become a member of The PGA of America?

Membership in The PGA of America is open to both men and women. As of mid 2001 there were slightly more than 19,000 fully certified members of The PGA of America and an additional 8,000 "apprentices" completing their studies. Of that membership, about 700 were women. (One of the benefits of The PGA of America membership is access to "Career Links," a placement and career service exclusive to members that also is available at www.pga.com.)

The PGA Golf Professional Training/Apprentice Program

The best-known PGA of America program is the "apprentice" program or Golf Professional Training Program (GPTP). This program allows aspiring professionals to work in the industry while they are completing their GPTP program. But before they can register for the GPTP program (which may be done online) students must pass the Player Ability Test mentioned above.

The GPTP curriculum consists of a series of seminars (which are now held in the new PGA education center in Port St. Lucie, Fla.), self-study programs and work as an "apprentice" in a golf facility. Materials for the program cost about $5,500, and students generally take several years to complete the three mandatory tests or "check points" of the GPTP.

Following is a list of the required courses and topics covered by the GPTP:

➢ Interpersonal Skills
➢ Golf Management I, II and III

JOB HUNTING TIPS

For junior and high school students:

As tough as the playing ability tests appear, with practice and good instruction they are not impossible to meet. Take advantage of the golf instruction offered by your school. If you are lucky, your school may have a golf team. Not everyone on the team begins as a good player, but they often end up as such.

Whether you become a great golfer or a golf pro, learning the game can open up many careers in the golf industry.

> ➤ Teaching Golf I, II III and IV
> ➤ Golf Club Design and Repair
> ➤ The Rules of Golf
> ➤ Turf Grass
> ➤ Golf Car Fleet Management
> ➤ Supervising and Delegating
> ➤ Career Enhancement
> ➤ Customer Relations

Additional electives include golf course design, caddie program management and public speaking.

The PGA of America now offers advanced certification – beyond the GPTP or PGM program – in specific areas: teaching, golf car fleet management, tournament operations, general management, golf operations, merchandising and rules.

The PGA of America Professional Golf Management Program – the four-year college route

In response to demand in the industry for golf pros who are college graduates, The PGA of America in 1975 established the "Professional Golf Management" program (PGM). Students can complete the required GPTP courses and apprenticeships while completing a four and one-half year college program leading to a bachelor of arts or bachelor of science degree.

The PGM program is currently offered at 11 colleges, listed below, and more are likely to come on board. By the end of 2001, approximately 2,000 students will have graduated from the PGM program.

Here is how the PGM program generally works:

1. Students must meet the general admission requirements of the college they plan to attend. Then, at the same time they are fulfilling the college's academic requirements (such as English and science classes), they will take the courses and self-study portions of the GPTP (listed above).

2. Each college's PGM program has its own playing ability requirements. Generally, a handicap index of eight or lower is a requirement for admission, but students are not required to pass The PGA of America's more rigorous Playing Ability Test before admission. Some PGM programs accept students with the expectation that during the program, with good instruction, they will become better golfers and will pass the PAT. (Women generally constitute less than 10 percent of each college's PGM program.)

One real benefit of these programs is that students gain real-life experience through apprenticeships, which count toward both their GPTP and academic requirements.

Here are some highlights and special features of the PGM programs:

(See the Appendix for contact information for each college.)

- **Arizona State University East's** PGM was founded in 1999. The suggested handicap index is eight for men and 10 for women. The program is housed in the Morrison School of Agribusiness. In addition to player development classes, the program offers expertise in food and beverage management for those interested in careers in golf facility management.

- **Campbell University** in Buies Creek, N.C., founded its PGM in 1999, and offers qualified students a unique opportunity to enter its "3/2" program – three years in the undergraduate college and two years in the business school. After five years, students earn MBAs from Campbell's School of Business.

- **Clemson University** in Clemson, S.C., accepted its first PGM class in the fall of 2001. Both men and women must have a handicap index of eight or lower to enter. The program offers a specialty to students interested in serving golfers with disabilities.

- **Coastal Carolina University** PGM was founded in 1999. The Conway, S.C., school is located outside of Myrtle Beach and had a freshman class in 2000 of 75, making it one of the largest programs. The PGM program is part of the Wall College of Business Administration, and students receive a B.S. in marketing.

- **Ferris State University** in Big Rapids, Mich., established in 1975, is the oldest PGM program. It also has the largest number of alumni – more than 1,000 – which is a plus for students looking for work-study positions and placement after graduation. Ferris is well respected for its marketing curriculum.

- **Florida State University** PGM, founded in 1999, limits class size and expects entering students to be able to pass The PGA of America's PAT within the first year. The program's concentration is in the hospitality industry. FSU's Dedman School of Hospitality is one of the top-ranked hospitality programs in the country.

- **Methodist College** in Fayetteville, N.C., has a business-oriented curriculum and is housed in the college's business school. Methodist admits women with a USGA handicap index of 12 or lower, and men must have a handicap index of eight or lower. Slightly more than 10 percent of the PGM students are women. The freshman class of 2000, with 86 students, was the largest freshman class in all of the PGM colleges.

- **Mississippi State University** PGM, also founded in 1975, offers degrees in turf management and golf course design, so students may take courses in these departments while in the PGM program. A unique work-study program offers students eight-month internships rather than just the summer work experience offered by most PGM programs.

- **North Carolina State** plans to inaugurate its PGM program with the freshman class of 2002. The program, located within the college's department of Parks, Recreation & Tourism Management, intends to focus on environmental concerns.

- **New Mexico State University** boasts the toughest admission requirements. Men should have a handicap of four or lower, women eight or lower – and all students must have a high school GPA of 3.0 or higher. One-fourth of the entering class in 2000 were women. The PGM program is located in the College of Business, Department of Marketing.

- **Penn State University** PGM was founded in 1991. It offers students curriculum opportunities in several of the university's highly respected programs: Recreation and Park Management, Business, Restaurant Management, and Turf Grass Management. The Penn State Turf Grass Management program is viewed by many in the industry as one of the top in the country.

How do I become a member of the LPGA Teaching and Club Professional Division?

The LPGA T&CP Division is the largest organization of female golf professionals in the country (www.lpga.com). Unlike The PGA of America programs, which offer apprentices the opportunity to work toward certification during college, most LPGA T&CP students have already completed college before starting the LPGA certification process.

As of 2001, there were more than 1,200 certified members of the LPGA T&CP. With women becoming increasingly interested in golf, there is a growing need for instructors who can relate to women golfers. LPGA-certified teachers are in great demand.

Admission to the LPGA program requires completing the PAT and carrying a handicap index of 12 or lower. It generally takes four years to complete all the requirements for the program. It is not uncommon for women to become certified by both The PGA of America and LPGA.

The four-year LPGA certification process features three levels of classification, culminating with a Class A credential. New programs are also in the works for national and regional workshops that focus on business skills, as well as career and leadership training.

What differentiates LPGA T&CP training from The PGA of America programs?

I asked Dr. Betsy Clark, Director of Education and Research for the LPGA T&CP Division that very question. Here is her answer:

"The basic difference between the PGA certification and the LPGA T&CP Division certification is their focus. The PGA focuses on facility management and operations, while the LPGA T&CP Division focuses on teacher training and the business of golf education. Instead of the GPTP program, LPGA members are required to take the LPGA National Education Program Series I, II and III prior to testing for Class A certification, and they also must complete other education electives. Each of the three programs is five days (40 hours) and focuses on teaching and learning theory, the business of golf education, teaching expertise, basic golf knowledge, communication, and equipment and club fitting. The program is progressive in nature moving from Class C apprentice to Class B and then Class A. The LPGA is the only organization that requires a "live" teaching evaluation as well as a written evaluation at the Class B and Class A levels."

What about attending an occupational college?

Another route to becoming a golf instructor is to attend a career or occupational college that specializes in golf. These two-year programs award an occupational associates degree that is approved by the Accrediting Council for Independent Colleges and Schools. (ACICS accreditation allows students to qualify for college loans and grants.)

Readers looking to move to the golf industry from other fields may find these schools appropriate for establishing – or refreshing – basic golf knowledge. Golf instruction is usually a major part of the curriculum, along with facility management and sales. Graduates may choose to work toward membership in The PGA of America and LPGA T&CP upon completion of these programs. Two established colleges are:

- **The Professional Golfer Career College**: Temecula, Calif.; www.progolfed.com; 800-877-4380. The school suggests that applicants who want to be club professionals have handicaps of 10 or lower – similar to The PGA of America and LPGA T&CP playing ability requirements. But students interested in working as general managers or in sales are admitted with handicaps as high as 20. The school offers placement services to all graduates and alumni.

- **The San Diego Golf Academy**: www.sdgagolf.com. The academy was founded in 1981. For the golf professional program, male applicants must have a handicap of eight or lower; women, a handicap of 15 or lower. For the golf management program, men's handicaps may be as high as 18; women's as high as 24. The school prepares students for the PGA Playing Ability Test and offers placement services. (SDGA operates programs in three other locations: The Golf Academy of the South in Orlando, Fla.; the Golf Academy of Arizona in Phoenix; and the Golf Academy of the Carolinas in Myrtle Beach, S.C.)

What if I don't have the time or money for college?

If you are a very good golfer and want to teach, you have other options.

The United States Golf Teachers Federation, www.usgtf.com, conducts a seven-day golf instruction and certification program in more than a dozen locations. The USGTF programs focus exclusively on teaching and instruction.

To pass the playing ability test for certification in this program, on the last two days of classes men must play two rounds of 83 or less (for a combined score of 166), and women must play two rounds 85 or less (for a combined score of 170) on par-72 championship courses. The PAT for senior men and women (age 50 to 59) is a few strokes easier. The program also requires successful completion of a written exam.

The USGTF program is especially suitable for those thinking of a second career in golf. The Professional Clubmakers Society (described in Chapter 7 – Careers in Retail) also recommends this certification program for club fitters who want to learn about swing technique.

A final option is on-the-job instruction. Many golf schools and academies train their own instructors. The golf school director may have developed his or her own methodology and prefers instructors who are trained in the school's methods from the start. Good golfers who are interested in teaching will generally be considered for positions.

Golf academies do not offer teaching certificates or degrees, but the experience looks good on a résumé. One way to identify golf schools is by reading golf magazines – many of their stories feature well known instructors and schools. More than fifty golf schools across the country also are listed in Shaw Guides, www.shawguides.com.

What if I want to be a Tour player?

You may recall that one of the criteria (identified in Chapter 1) for a career to be included in this book was that there had to be a significant number of positions available. Every year, hundreds of men and women try to qualify to play on the tours. Only a handful do, which is why not much space is devoted to this career.

But, this *is* a book about golf. Millions of people watch PGA and LPGA Tour professionals on television, and probably thousands aspire to join their ranks.

Have you ever wondered exactly what "turning pro" means? It means that a golfer has given up his or her amateur status by deciding to accept significant financial prizes and rewards for play. (Golfers cannot retain amateur status if they accept significant prize money.) It also means that they will spend many hours traveling to tournaments and practicing golf.

Golfers who turn pro and qualify for one of the professional tours (usually by scoring well in scheduled qualifying tournaments) are betting that they can make a living at golf through prize winnings or through corporate sponsorships.

If you are an excellent golfer and want to know more about the process of qualifying for the professional tours, visit the LPGA or PGA Tour Web sites, www.pgatour.com and www.lpga.com, for information on their qualifying schools, which are usually held in the fall.

CAREERS TO EXPLORE

DIRECTOR OF GOLF

A good way to think about the duties and responsibilities of the *director of golf* is to think of the position as "general manager" of everything connected with golf at a facility. Traditionally, the director of golf is usually a member of The PGA of America or LPGA T&CP Division.

The director of golf usually begins his or her career as an *assistant golf professional*, then works at least three to five years as a *head golf professional* before promotion to director of golf. Though most directors of golf are good players, the role is managerial, and more time is spent in the office than on the course.

The median salary of a director of golf in the U.S., at a daily fee facility in 1999 was $51,200 (source: National Golf Foundation). Salaries in the Sun Belt states are significantly higher. This figure does not include additional income from golf lessons, golf cart operations or merchandise sales.

Career Close-up: HEAD GOLF PROFESSIONAL

OVERVIEW: The duties and responsibilities of the *head golf professional* – sometimes referred to as simply the *golf professional* or *head pro* – depend on the size and type of facility.

At a private course, the head pro may report directly to the owner (or board of directors), or, if at a large private course, to the director of golf. At a large daily fee or resort, the head pro often reports to the director of golf (explained above) or the general manager. At a mu-

---

JOB HUNTING TIPS:

Ask about job responsibilities

Until about 1980, the most senior position at a golf course was the head golf professional. As the industry expanded, The PGA of America and golf facilities recognized the need for two distinct positions at a golf facility.

One, the director of golf, assumes overall management and financial responsibility for all golf operations, including course maintenance, food and beverage, and marketing. The second position, the head golf professional, generally reports to the director of golf and interacts with customers on a day-to-day basis.

Accordingly, there is a certain degree of overlap between the titles "general manager," "director of golf," and "head golf professional." When interviewing for a position, it is always a good idea to inquire about actual duties and responsibilities.

nicipal course, the head professional may function like a director of golf and have broad management responsibilities.

The head pro may play quite a bit of golf with members or customers – or he or she may play very little. Many, but not all, head golf professionals have worked their way through The PGA of America or LPGA apprentice programs and have spent time working in a pro shop and giving lessons.

DUTIES: The head golf professional is in charge of the golf operations of a facility. The following operations are common to almost all golf facilities and are the core responsibilities of the head professional, who may be managing a staff of more than 50: bag drop, tee time registration, retail shops, golf car fleet, caddie program, starters and rangers, practice range, bag cleaning and storage, food cart or snack bar, tournament management and golf instruction.

The job of head golf professional is one of the most customer-oriented professions in the industry. "It's all about service, service, service," as one head pro told us. As discussed in the Chapter 7 – Careers in Retail, at some facilities the head golf professional manages the pro shop and receives its profits.

Additional responsibilities for the head pro – especially at smaller facilities without a director of golf – may include the following:

- Promoting the facility and creating golf packages for conferences.
- Preparing an annual budget and interacting regularly with the owner or general manager.

SALARY RANGE: Salaries for head golf pros vary among private, daily fee, and municipal courses. According to NGF studies, the median salary of a head pro in 1999 at the various course types, ranged between $35,000 and $42,000, excluding income from lessons, cars and pro shop operations.

JOB OPPORTUNITIES: The survey responses we received suggest that career opportunities are good to very good. There are also plenty of opportunities for those who want to leverage experience as head golf professionals into senior management roles with golf management companies.

EDUCATION & TRAINING: A college degree with a major in business or marketing is recommended, and should be augmented by specific golf professional training. Head professionals report that accounting and business planning are also valuable skills. Although it is not essential to have formal training or certification from a golf management school, a degree from a PGM program is recommended because the job market is highly competitive.

ENTRY-LEVEL POSITIONS: Every head professional admits to having "paid dues" working long hours as an assistant golf professional, which means lots of time behind the counter in the pro shop or helping with tournaments. Many say that their apprentice programs helped them understand the importance of customer service.

GOLF ABILITY & INTEREST: It is very important to like golf and golfers, since this position involves so much interaction with them. A head golf professional is expected to be an expert on many aspects of the game. And he or she is often called upon to participate in tournaments and marketing activities.

SPECIAL SKILLS & PERSONAL TRAITS: This is a very service-oriented profession, so one must be outgoing. Management and human resources skills are very important.

CAREER LADDER & PROMOTION PROSPECTS: Promotion prospects are good for people who are self-starters, are motivated and who have good management skills. There are many opportunities for management positions with golf management companies.

SALARY: Assistant golf professional positions offer traditionally low salaries. In 1999 the range was from $15,000 to $26,000 (source: National Golf Foundation).

> **SOUND BITES FROM GOLF PROS**
> **Positive**
> "It's a fun career."
> "It means making a living at something you enjoy."
> **Negative:**
> "Hours are extremely long."
> "There's little family time."

DIRECTOR OF INSTRUCTION

Although most head golf professionals are qualified to teach, they spend more time supervising overall operations than giving lessons. Nevertheless, some golf professionals love to teach and specialize exclusively in instruction.

A career as a ***director of instruction*** or ***golf instructor*** may be one of the "purist" professions in the golf industry. The positions are filled by people who enjoy teaching and are not generally looking to be promoted to head golf professionals or directors of golf; the management responsibilities would keep them from what they love to do.

Some facilities prefer to hire instructors as independent contractors. This is often the case at municipal facilities, where costs are kept to a minimum. Working as an independent contractor offers the instructor scheduling flexibility, but reduces the employment benefits he or she might receive.

A full-time instructor at a busy facility can earn more than $80,000 annually. Entry-level positions start at $25,000, and the average salary is around $50,000.

INDUSTRY LEADER Q&A

An interview with Gary Wiren, Ph.D., Chairman and Founder, Golf Around the World, Inc., located in Lake Park, Fla. Golf Around the World, Inc., manufactures and distributes golf training aids via direct sales to golf club and teaching professionals and Internet golf sites.

Q. **How did you hone your effectiveness as a teacher?**

A. It was a educational process. There are primarily four ways I've learned: From students through trial and error, from peers through formal education, through reading golf books, and by playing and practicing.

Q. **What's your teaching methodology?**

A. It's about much more than swing mechanics; it's more holistic – mind and body mechanics. In teaching, I try to make instruction fun and more interesting with stories and examples, because people learn better when they're relaxed. The poorest way to teach a motor skill is by simply talking. The best way is kinesthetically and visually, which I emphasize.

Q. **What does it take to be a good teacher?**

A. You have to have a love, and great empathy, for people. You have to care more about others than yourself. If you're a great player and always worried about your own game, you probably are not going to be a great teacher. Great teachers are also life-long learners.

Q. **What would you advise people about learning the technical side of teaching golf?**

A. You can't get enough training. Learn some anatomy and kinesiology, go to seminars and look into professional programs like those offered by The PGA of America and the LPGA. It takes a lot of time and effort to become competent, and the financial payoff may not be great. But the other rewards from being in the golf business continue to attract people.

Q. How has instruction changed over the years?

A. Teachers are much better informed about mechanics because there are more resources available to them via video, the Internet, television, and, increasingly, books and articles on instruction. Couple these things with better teaching and learning aids, and better analytical tools, and you have better informed teachers. Though teaching is more competitive today, it still can be financially rewarding for those who excel. So strive to be the best!

CHAPTER NINE

Careers in Tour Management and Event Planning

"Event management is really about working behind the scenes. If it's done right, the participants don't know how much work went into it. It's not a social occupation. It really takes someone who is able to work on his own, in the background."

> Roger Yaffe, President,
> RMY Management Group, L.L.C.

In This Chapter

- What are the different types of golf events?
- What are the career opportunities in event management?
- How do I find a job with a professional tour?
- Where can I learn more about tour operations?
- Learn about the following positions:
    Tournament Director
    Meeting Planner
- Interview with Roger M. Yaffe, President, RMY Management Group, L.L.C.

In this chapter, our career tour meets the golf tours. But we won't be talking about playing in tournaments; we will be talking about managing tournament events.

What are the different types of golf tournaments and events?

Nearly 40,000 spectators attend each day of major professional golf tournament events. Millions more watch the events on television. Televised golf has increased the number of golf fans, the number of golfers and the number of golf occupations.

In addition to the professional tournaments, however, there are thousands of amateur tournaments and corporate golf events. A *Directory of Golf Tournament Directors* compiled by Crittenden Magazines, a publisher of golf newsletters and magazines, lists more than 900 **tournament directors** associated with more than 200 companies, organizations and associations that sponsor or manage golf tournaments. (The directory is available for $287 from Crittenden Golf at 877-465-3462; www.crittendengolf.com.)

This sector of the industry is so large that it is helpful to break it into three broad categories:

- Tournaments for professional golfers.
- Tournaments sponsored by golf associations for serious amateur golfers.
- Tournaments for recreational golfers, including charity tournaments and meetings and corporate events.

Who sponsors tournaments?

- **USGA CHAMPIONSHIPS:**

The United States Golf Association, www.usga.org, conducts three events that are considered our national championships: the U.S. Open, U.S. Women's Open, and U.S. Senior Open.

The USGA also sponsors 14 national amateur championships, from tournaments for juniors (under the age of 18) to tournaments for senior men (over the age of 55) and senior women (over the age of 50). Many of today's golf stars began their careers playing USGA amateur championships. The USGA amateur events are professionally managed – by either USGA staff or outside management companies – but rely heavily on volunteers. Several events, such as the U.S. Amateur and U.S. Women's Amateur, receive significant television coverage.

- **PGA TOUR EVENTS:**

The PGA TOUR (a separate organization from The PGA of America) sponsors or co-sponsors more than 50 tournaments each year. Local tournament committees runs these events with the financial backing of corporate sponsors, such as Honda and AT&T, whose names become part of the tournament titles (the Honda Classic and AT&T Pebble Beach National Pro-Am, for example). In additional to offering purses, or money to players, PGA TOUR events raise millions of dollars for charity.

The PGA TOUR also manages two other tours. The Senior PGA TOUR sponsors 35 to 40 tournaments a year for men 50 and older, and the BUY.COM TOUR (formerly the Hogan Tour and NIKE TOUR) is a "developmental tour" that helps pros gain the experience to qualify for the PGA TOUR. It has about 35 annual tournaments.

Besides sponsoring tournaments, the PGA TOUR operates several other businesses: PGA TOUR Productions, the television and video arm of the tour; the Tournament Players Clubs – approximately 20 golf clubs, some of which serve as tournament sites; a PGA TOUR Web site; and a string of PGA TOUR golf shops. A good entry-level position with any of these PGA TOUR divisions, www.pgatour.com, can open many doors for you.

• **LPGA TOUR EVENTS:**

The Ladies Professional Golf Association (LPGA) – often with financial backing of corporations – sponsors about 40 professional tournament events a year (www.lpga.com). Most are in the U.S., but international venues are receiving increased attention. The developmental tour of the LPGA is the SBC Futures Tour – often referred to as simply the Futures Tour – which sponsors about 20 events in the U.S. (www.futurestour.com). The Futures Tour Web site posts job opportunities.

The LPGA tournaments are managed more on a local basis than from the LPGA headquarters in Florida. Use the Web sites to identify the local tournament director and inquire about positions and internships.

New to the LPGA Tour roster is the Women's Senior Tour, www.wsgtour.com, featuring 25 well-known players including Nancy Lopez and Jane Blalock. The Women's Senior Tour may appeal to corporate and special events because it will "custom build" a tournament for a sponsor. This could be very exciting work for those on the ground floor of this new tournament venture.

Tournaments sponsored by golf associations

Many golf associations, discussed in Chapter 2 – Careers in Golf Associations, sponsor tournaments and maintain permanent tournament operations staffs. (Most state golf associations, for example, sponsor tournaments for serious amateur golfers.) Positions generally require experience in tournament operations. State golf associations can be located at www.usga.org.

The American Junior Golf Association, www.ajga.org, holds more than 60 tournaments a year. In addition to hiring tournament directors, it also offers summer internship programs in tournament operations.

What occupations exist in professional tour management?

Let's look at the pro tours first. Most professional tournaments – those that consist of players who have given up their amateur status and expect to make a living from prize money – have a permanent staff that is augmented by contract employees, consultants and volunteers. There are six key functions or positions for most professional tournaments.

Most of these titles will oversee several assistants:

1. ***Tournament director:*** The chief executive officer of the tournament. The positions below report to him or her.
2. ***Operations manager:*** In charge of food and beverage services and hospitality for sponsors, guests and spectators.
3. ***Sales promotions:*** Handles corporate sponsorships and merchandise sales.
4. ***Client services coordinator:*** Manages sponsor-related events.
5. ***Media relations:*** Responsible for public relations and news releases.
6. ***Rules officials:*** Makes sure tees, fairways, hazards and spectator areas are properly marked and that the event is staffed by Rules officials.

How do I find a job with a professional Tour?

If you would like to work in a paid entry-level position for a professional tournament, the best route is to contact the ***tournament director***. Many positions are filled months in advance of the tournament date, but there are always a few last-minute openings. If you are bold enough to knock on a tournament director's door and are prepared to take any job offered – even running errands – you may get lucky. Here are several suggestions for finding tournament directors in your area:

* The PGA TOUR Tournaments Association Web site, www.pgatta.com, is an umbrella administration of 50 men's professional tournaments – most of which are sponsored by the PGA TOUR. One advantage of the association's Web site is that it provides links to each of the 50 tournament Web sites. (See www.hondaclassic.com for an example.)

* The "Tournaments" section of the PGA TOUR Web site, www.pgatour.com, lists PGA TOUR, Senior TOUR, and BUY.COM TOUR tournament schedules. The Web site of the LPGA, www.lpga.com, also provides a schedule of its tournaments. You can contact courses or tournament management offices and ask for the names and numbers of tournament directors.

* The USGA Web site, www.usga.org, also lists tournaments and locations for its championships. The "amateur" page allows you to search for tournaments by state. Your state golf associations likely have similar tournament schedules posted on their Web sites.

* The International Association of Golf Administrators, www.iaga.org, was created in 1968 to improve communications between golf associations. Its Web site includes an employment page that includes tournament operations positions.

JOB HUNTING TIPS:

Start as a volunteer

Many professional tournaments require hundreds of volunteers, so volunteering is a good way to build your résumé. Most tournaments offer training for newcomers. (A note of warning: It is not unusual for volunteers to be required to purchase a golf outfit or uniform – up to $100. Of course, you get to keep the uniform after the event.)

The employment Web site www.golfingcareers. com posts positions for volunteers.

What about recreational golf events?

Not all golf tournaments are for professionals or serious amateurs. Every year thousands of events take place for recreational golfers. ***Event planners*** specialize in planning events for recreational golfers.

Some clarification may be helpful to distinguish recreational golfers from amateurs, although every "non-professional" golfer is by definition an "amateur," the word "amateur" generally implies a serious golfer who plays in competitive events. Of course, some recreational golfers periodically test their skills in amateur events, but most recreational golfers play primarily for social, business and leisure reasons.

Corporate golf outings and fund-raising tournaments have become common at many facilities. In fact, it's hard for a golfer not to be invited to at least one special event each season. These events range from small corporate outings to large fund-raising tournaments with several hundred participants.

If the event sponsors have dedicated events management departments, or a talented group of volunteers, they may be able to plan entire events in-house. Career opportunities exist in the events management departments of many large corporations.

In contrast, many charity tournaments rely heavily on volunteers. The Rally For a Cure tournaments, which raise funds for the Susan G. Komen Breast Cancer Foundation and are held at hundreds of courses in the U.S., send an easy-to-use tournament kit to sponsoring clubs. The clubs' chairmen usually become volunteer "tournament directors."

Recently, however, as events planning and promotion has become more sophisticated, many organizations have come to rely on outside expertise from ***professional meeting planners***.

What are meeting planners?

The meeting planning industry is an outgrowth of the larger hospitality or hotel industry. As hotel convention business has grown, "meeting planning" has become a specialized occupation.

(The hospitality industry is a "mega" industry comprised of hotels, motels, clubs, restaurants, tourism, cruise lines and theme parks. The hospitality industry has its own career Web site: www.hcareers.com, where some golf facilities post jobs.)

The largest association of meeting planners is the Professional Convention Management Association, www.pcma.org. The organization has local chapters and offers self-study programs and seminars on meeting-planning skills. An advanced program resulting in a Professional Meeting Planner certificate (PMP) is available. An online PMP course costs about $300; the Web site includes scholarship information. The PCMA also offers numerous publications.

Tournament directors specializing in recreational golf events also have formed an association – the National Association of Golf Tournament Directors, www.nagtd.com. The NAGTD held its first week-long education program in 2001. The program is open to both new and experienced event managers.

CAREERS TO EXPLORE

Career Close-up: TOURNAMENT DIRECTOR – PROFESSIONAL GOLF EVENTS

DUTIES: A *tournament director's* duties resemble those of a project manager. Since a tournament is run within a specific time frame, a tournament director can't miss deadlines for getting bleachers up, cameras in place, ropes up on the course, etc. Tournament directors only have one chance to get everything right.

A tournament director is usually responsible for a staff of six to 10, but by tournament week, he or she will be indirectly responsible for thousands of volunteers and workers. Several key senior directors usually report to the tournament director.

SALARY RANGE: The salary of tournament directors is not high. Entry-level salaries may be less than $20,000 annually.

JOB OPPORTUNITIES: Turnover is infrequent, so opportunities are limited with major professional tournaments. Opportunities are better within associations.

EDUCATION & TRAINING: Many tournament directors have worked as golf professionals, and most golf professional programs include courses on tournament operations. The PGA of America offers a certification program specializing in tournament operations. Prior experience in an entry-level position is also important.

ENTRY-LEVEL POSITIONS: Barry Palm, executive director of the PGA TOUR Tournament Associations advises newcomers to "take any job you can get." Entry-level positions may include running errands, checking visitor passes at a corporate sponsor's booth or faxing press releases.

GOLF ABILITY & INTEREST: Golf knowledge is essential at the top tournament management level. For professional events, tournament directors must also be familiar with the expectations and needs of professional golfers.

SPECIAL SKILLS & PERSONAL TRAITS: The tournament director must be able to manage a staff while keeping track of large and small details, such as crowd control, food concessions, signs and lavatories.

Career Close-up: MEETING PLANNER –
TOURNAMENT DIRECTOR OF
NON-PROFESSIONAL EVENTS

OVERVIEW: *Meeting planners* – also referred to as tournament directors or *event managers* – may be employed by corporations, resorts or charities, or they may be self-employed and head their own firms.

Being in charge of a corporate or charity outing may not be as complex as running a nationally televised tournament, but it has challenges. The meeting planner generally does not have a large staff and wears many hats, including that of public relations director. There is more oversight of minor details, such food and prizes.

DUTIES: Unlike for professional tournaments, where one course is usually "home" to a particular event, the meeting planner is often asked to select appropriate locations for events.

The meeting planner may also be asked to schedule conferences, meetings and travel plans, as well as the tournament format and prizes.

SALARY RANGE: Salaries vary significantly since many event management firms are owner-operated. The average annual salary is $50,000, but the president of an established firm can earn more than $100,000.

JOB OPPORTUNITIES: According to the meeting planners and event managers we interviewed, opportunities are excellent. Golf continues to be a popular venue for business and charities events.

EDUCATION & TRAINING: Many meeting planners say on-the-job training is invaluable. But several associations offer programs and seminars to get you started. See the Club Managers Association of America Web site, www.cmaa.org, and the Professional Convention Management Association Web site, www.pcma.org. If you plan to work in the hospitality industry, you will be exposed to event management in your convention services training.

ENTRY-LEVEL POSITIONS: Take any job that provides experience managing an event. Do not overlook volunteer organizations.

GOLF ABILITY & INTEREST: Since your clients are not usually golf experts or professionals, you do not have to be an expert golfer. However, the meeting planner often coordinates with resident golf professionals, so it is important to have a general knowledge of the

---

SOUND BITES FROM MEETING PLANNERS

Positive

"This is a great job for an 'organizer.'"

"I learn something new every day."

Negative:

"It's a somewhat thankless job. When everything goes right, nobody notices; when things go wrong, they do."

"There's a misconception that this job is glamorous and easy."

game.

SPECIAL SKILLS & PERSONAL TRAITS: Most meeting planners list "attention to detail" as critical. But flexibility is also important as bad weather, scheduling conflicts, and other problems arise frequently. You must be assertive, but as one planner suggested, you can't be a "Type A" personality.

CAREER LADDER & PROMOTION PROSPECTS: Many meeting planners have worked in the hotel and resort – or hospitality – industry.

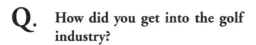

INDUSTRY LEADER Q&A

An interview with Roger M. Yaffe, President, RMY Management Group, L.L.C., an event management company.

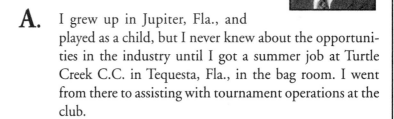

Q. **How did you get into the golf industry?**

A. I grew up in Jupiter, Fla., and played as a child, but I never knew about the opportunities in the industry until I got a summer job at Turtle Creek C.C. in Tequesta, Fla., in the bag room. I went from there to assisting with tournament operations at the club.

Q. **What would you tell someone who wants to get into tournament management?**

A. Seek out a position that allows you to get the broadest perspective. Working for an association, even on a local or regional level is a great way to break in. I worked at the National Golf Foundation in the membership department, answering phones and talking to manufacturers, facilities, students, etc. I was exposed to all aspects of the industry.

Q. Event management seems like a high-profile career where you're surrounded by golf celebrities. What's the real story?

A. Event management is really about working behind the scenes. If it's done right, the participants don't know how much work went into it. It's not a social occupation. It really takes someone who is able to work on his own, in the background.

Q. What else does it take to be a successful event manager?

A. You have to be willing to work extremely long hours. You're up at 4 a.m. and not back in your room until late for days at a time. You also have to be a good negotiator, creative with a budget and forceful. When you're at an event, and the host says you can't do something that must get done, you have to know how to get what you want.

Q. What would you look for in a job candidate?

A. Someone who is extremely detail-oriented. You have to be able to set priorities, manage projects and remember details.

Q. What's the most exciting aspect of planning an event?

A. When you've been putting in the hours and effort, you feel a lot of satisfaction the moment the event begins. Your job is 98 percent done, and you're there just to manage unexpected issues. The event takes on a life of its own.

CHAPTER TEN

Careers in Marketing and Public Relations

"When we're hiring, we're looking for the right personality. We want to find people who have basic PR and special events skills and will teach them about golf."

Karen Moraghan, President,
Hunter Public Relations/Special Events (HPR, Inc.)

In This Chapter

- What is marketing?
- What marketing careers are available in the golf industry?
- How is marketing different from sales?
- What is public relations?
- What is a marketing consultant?
- Learn about the following positions:
    Director of Marketing
    Public Relations Director
    Media Coordinator
- Interview with Karen Moraghan, President, Hunter Public Relations/ Special Events (HPR, Inc.)

We have toured golf courses and facilities, manufacturing and retail sales, golf instruction and golf events. The common feature of all these subjects is that they need customers. What good is a course if no one plays there? What good is a product if no one buys it? And what good is a golf tournament if no one enters it?

This tour stop focuses on attracting and keeping customers.

Occupations involving customer service have already been described a bit in Chapter 7 – Careers in Retail. What's different about the positions described in this chapter is that they seldom require direct contact with end customers.

What is marketing?

Marketing involves understanding what types of products or services customers want – or think they want – and then producing, pricing, promoting and distributing those products accordingly.

In business, a "market" is a group of customers who have a specific need and who are willing to purchase a product – or service – to satisfy that need. Generally, the broader the product or service, the broader the market, and the narrower the product's use, the narrower the market. Narrow markets (described in more detail below) are sometimes referred to as "niche" markets. Customers with similar needs, attributes and purchasing patterns are sometimes referred to as a market "segment."

Here are examples of marketing activities for both broad and narrow markets in the golf industry:

- The market for the broad category of golf clubs (all types and prices) is any person who has an interest in golf clubs and the money to purchase them. This market has millions of potential customers of all ages, golf skills and incomes.

  For this broad market segment, a ***director of marketing*** would consider advertising his or her company's clubs in a newspaper that reaches thousands of diverse readers. The director of marketing might decide the price of the clubs should be affordable – perhaps a few hundred dollars. The director might also advise the company to distribute the items in well-trafficked stores – perhaps the mass merchandisers described in the Chapter 7. But before actually spending money on advertising or distribution, the director might want to observe a few "focus groups" of potential customers to see how best to reach them.

- The market for high-performance $500 drivers is more limited. It consists of golfers whose desire for high performance drivers – probably serious or competitive golfers – and who can afford the product.

  The director of marketing's approach will be quite different than for a broad market. Advertising in publications that reach affluent households might be more effective. This market segment may be more knowledgeable about golf, and the promotions will probably include plenty of information on club technology and design.

  These examples involve golf clubs, but the marketing tactics could apply to any product or service – from marketing tee times at a course to marketing golf balls.

What is the difference between marketing and sales?

Although marketing and sales are often grouped together, they really are different disciplines. Marketing focuses on *understanding* the customer; sales focuses on *influencing, persuading, urging and convincing* a customer.

Those involved in marketing must understand how a product or service will be sold, and those in sales have to understand the marketing decisions – such as price and promotions – involved in bringing the product to the marketplace.

Most businesses strive for good communication between sales and marketing departments, which explains why many companies group the two together. You may see a position advertised as ***marketing and sales*** or the title ***vice president of marketing and sales***. But now that you know the difference between the two, you will be better able to evaluate positions to fit your skills.

What are the careers in marketing?

The director of marketing is a key marketing position within a company. The director of marketing may have several ***assistant marketing directors*** responsible for specific projects.

The ***director of market research*** is a specialized position. As competition increases, businesses invest more in market research before undertaking projects.

Another marketing specialty of increasing importance is the ***director of public relations*** (see below).

What are the four "P's" of marketing?

A helpful way to understand marketing careers is to think of the four key dimensions of marketing – sometimes called the four "P's": Product, Price, Place and Promotion.

- **Product:** Developing a product involves both market research – understanding customer needs – and product design and engineering. In the golf equipment sector, where scientific research is a critical element of product development, product development is often the responsibility of the manufacturing department. (See Chapter 6 – Careers in Manufacturing for more about ***directors of product development***.) In the resort side of the industry, the ***director of convention sales*** may design convention packages – a type of product – that offer meeting rooms, hotel rooms and tee times.

- **Price:** One of the principal roles of marketing involves pricing a product or service. Strong financial skills are required to develop projected costs and revenues for new products. The director of market research may test-market products at various prices.

- **Place (also referred to as distribution):** Marketing departments have to consider where and how a product will be sold. Different methods of distribution result in different expenses and profit projections. For example, if a new sales force must be trained, that cost must be figured into the price of the product.

- **Promotion:** The ways in which a product will be advertised and promoted are traditional marketing issues. A ***director of advertising*** or *director of public relations* may handle the job. The *director of advertising* at a company that manufactures golf equipment, for example, has to select the style of advertisements, and the types of media in which they will run. Most companies and organizations do not create their own advertisements. They rely on advertising firms where *account executives* manage and oversee the production of advertisements.

What is brand management?

A "brand" is a name, term or design that identifies a product, and more important, differentiates it from competitors. A company's image can be built around its brand, and brands often develop powerful customer loyalty. Customers often are willing to pay a premium for brands they respect and value.

Many sales and marketing positions require specific experience in "brand management." One of the best ways to acquire experience in brand management is to work for a big consumer company outside of the golf industry.

What is public relations?

Public relations is a marketing function closely linked to promotion, but "PR" is different from traditional advertising. Media-generated stories hold more influence over potential customers than do paid advertisements. This is why many companies promote their products through both advertising and public relations campaigns. The director of public relations creates "press releases" and "news," which he or she distributes to the media in the hopes that they will forward the message.

Here is an example of how public relations can be used to promote a new golf resort. The resort may schedule a media day or a tournament with well-known golfers in the hopes of generating publicity. The public relations department or consultant will issue invitations and press releases, hoping that reporters will attend the event and write or broadcast stories about the new resort.

What is a public relations consultant?

Another common career in marketing is the position of *marketing* or *public relations consultant*.

Many companies do not have enough in-house work to maintain a permanent marketing staff. But they many need help with advertising brochures or developing special promotions. In contracting with independent consultants, companies get marketing expertise without having to pay annual salaries and benefits.

Consultants may have several assistants, or they may work solo. Like independent sales representatives (Chapter 6 – Careers with Manufacturers) and freelance writers (Chapter 11 – Careers in the Media), they enjoy scheduling flexibility.

Where can I learn more about marketing?

Many colleges have majors in marketing or business administration. Several of the college PGM programs described in Chapter 8 offer a concentration in marketing. Many senior marketing positions require a master's in business administration.

If you do not have a business degree, you may still be able to work in the field. Many companies will hire motivated college graduates and train them as marketing assistants.

What types of companies and associations offer marketing jobs?

Every company or association that is interested in its customers has a marketing function – even if it does not have an official marketing department or director. Here are some examples:

➤ Associations conduct market research to identify services that will attract new members.

➤ Developers conduct market research to determine whether there will be enough customers to support a new golf facility.

➤ Golf course construction firms prepare advertising brochures to attract clients.

➤ Manufacturers develop distribution and pricing plans for their products.

➤ Golf associations promote tournaments in the media.

➤ Golf resorts employ public relations experts to attract media attention.

How do you know you will be good at marketing?

Alison Wagonfeld, an experienced marketing executive, graduated from Harvard Business School with a passion for both marketing and golf. Having worked as director of marketing for several start-up companies in Silicon Valley, Calif., she offers the following advice:

1. **You should enjoy learning about the customer**. A good marketer enjoys conducting and analyzing market research about potential customers and market size. This research often involves assimilating data from various sources. For example, if you were marketing a new

line of golf clothes, it would be important to survey retailers about when and how often people are buying current designs. You might also use focus groups to find out what types of golf clothes certain people want to buy – and at what price. Then, you would draw conclusions to help you position your new clothing line.

2. **You should be comfortable working in a team.** Marketing departments often interact with sales, finance, product development and customer service departments. As a result, a good marketer thrives on pulling together teams and keeping each informed. Often, the marketer takes on the role of team leader. It is important that a marketer enjoy working with others.

3. **You should consider yourself a creative person.** In most organizations, the marketing staff is responsible for promoting a product or service through advertising and promotions. In large companies, such as Nike or Callaway, a marketing person may hire an agency to help. Successful promotions often involve coming up with exciting new ways to present products or services. Successful marketers like to be involved in this creative process.

4. **You should have strong written and verbal communication skills.** A marketer spends much of his or her day communicating. Sometimes this communication is with customers in the form of advertising and promotions; other times it means conveying a vision for a product to the rest of the staff. Strong marketers are skilled at making presentations, as well as drafting memos and product brochures.

CAREERS TO EXPLORE

Career Close-up: DIRECTOR OF MARKETING – GOLF RESORT

OVERVIEW: Most large resorts employ a marketing department, whether to attract customers to play their courses, rent their convention facilities or buy their vacation homes.

Resorts may be owned by a single investor or developer, but more often they are owned by a hotel chain or golf management company. Working at a multi-property resort has positives and negatives.

On the positive side, there may be many opportunities for promotion. Large companies may have *local*, *regional and national marketing directors*. In addition, you may be working for a company that has a strong brand name – such as Hyatt Hotels & Resorts or Pebble Beach Resorts.

On the negative side, however, hotels and golf management companies are very focused on the bottom line. There is pressure on the marketing departments to position the company for strong sales and profits. An ad campaign may look great, but stockholders and investors will measure the its success in terms of increased hotel occupancy and tee times.

DUTIES: The full range of marketing activities – the Four P's listed on page 105 – are under the supervision of the *director of marketing*.

SALARY: The director of marketing at a large resort can earn between $80,000 and $120,000 annually. The entry-level position of *marketing assistant* begins around $30,000 a year. Mid-level salaries range from $60,000 to $70,000.

JOB OPPORTUNITIES: Opportunities are very good because marketing is an increasingly important part of the industry. Expect to work long hours in entry-level positions. Promotions usually require moving from one company to another.

EDUCATION: The minimum requirement is a college degree. Majors in business, marketing or hospitality are desirable. An MBA is becoming important.

ENTRY-LEVEL POSITIONS: Any staff position in the marketing department of a golf facility or hotel is a good place to start. Golf professionals who want to transfer from the pro shop to the marketing department can take advantage of marketing workshops and seminars offered by The PGA of America.

GOLF SKILLS & KNOWLEDGE: Many directors of marketing become involved in showing off the resort to the media and to potential customers – especially to conventions and group business.

> **JOB HUNTING TIPS:**
>
> **Explore hotel training programs**
>
> Most large hotel chains have excellent training programs and welcome college graduates with good communication skills.

Career Close-up: DIRECTOR OF MARKETING – ASSOCIATION

DUTIES: The *director of marketing* (also referred to as *director of communication*) for a golf association is responsible for the entire marketing efforts of the association, including the development of membership services, advertising, publications and Web sites, and public relations.

In some associations, there will be directors for each of the various departments such as *director of membership*, *publications director*, etc.

SALARY RANGE: Salaries vary widely depending on the size of the association. Directors of large associations with big advertising and publication budgets earn top annual salaries, which may be as high as $85,000. More common are salaries in the $40,000 range. Not-for-profit associations generally pay less than for-profit businesses.

EDUCATION: The recommended education is a college degree with a major in either business administration, marketing or journalism. An MBA is helpful and often required for positions with large companies.

JOB OPPORTUNITIES: Within golf associations, opportunities for marketing positions are limited. Only the large or growing associations have the resources to keep large marketing staffs. But marketing experience within associations transfers well to positions in the for-profit sector. Review the employment opportunities page of the International Association of Golf Administrators, www.iaga.org, for marketing opportunities.

GOLF ABILITY & INTEREST: Golf knowledge is very helpful in marketing jobs. It is much easier to understand the customer if you understanding the game they are playing.

DIRECTOR OF MARKETING – MANUFACTURER

With all the manufacturers in the golf industry – from ball and club makers, to turf equipment and software companies – you might think that marketing positions are plentiful. In fact, except for very large manufacturers who can afford permanent marketing staffs, many manufacturers outsource their marketing functions to advertising firms or merge them within their sales departments.

Therefore, if you want to pursue a marketing position in the industry, your best opportunities will be with large golf manufacturing companies. The catch is that most of them are looking for marketers with experience. To gain that experience, seek out entry-level marketing positions outside the golf industry. (Many key marketing positions require a bachelor's degree in marketing or an MBA.)

The director of marketing for a large manufacturer has broad responsibilities that may include establishing the company's strategic direction, developing advertising, public relations and regional marketing programs, and supervising a large staff to execute the plans.

In reviewing job postings, remember that marketing positions are often described as sales positions. If you have marketing skills, you may want to consider a sales position so long as it has some marketing component, with the hope that you will be able to make contacts within the company and move into a marketing position.

Several of the large golf manufacturers list employment opportunities on their Web sites. A good example is Nike, Inc. at www.nikegolf.com.

PUBLIC RELATIONS EXECUTIVE/CONSULTANT

Most companies and organizations in the golf industry cannot afford to maintain a permanent public relations staff. They rely instead on outside consulting firms.

The primary duties of public relations professionals are to:

> ➤ Identify the audience or market a business is trying to reach.

> ➤ Identify the media – newspapers, magazines, television stations – that reach that market.

> ➤ Identify events or "news" that will be attractive to the media.

> ➤ Write and distribute news releases to the media.

> ➤ Plan events that the media will attend.

> ➤ Follow up with friendly reminders to the media.

Although a college degree is advised, there is no specific major that prepares you for public relations work. A background in English is helpful because much of the work involves writing and communication.

The skills associated with public relations are patience, friendliness, inquisitiveness and creativity. A playing knowledge of golf is essential.

A good entry-level position in public relations is that of *media coordinator*. Large golf resorts and new facilities receive requests from writers and reporters who would like to visit. The media coordinator makes the arrangements, from reserving the best hotel rooms to securing tee times.

Another entry-level job is the position of *account executive* at a PR firm – even if not in the golf industry. You may be asked to make telephone calls and send faxes, but if you are attentive, you will learn to write news releases and place stories. Test out your skills and build your résumé by offering to write press releases for a local charity tournament.

Salaries for *administrative assistants* in PR firms begin around $22,000. Account executives earn more than $30,000. Senior executives of successful firms can expect to earn more than $75,000.

Following are interviews with two public relations executives. One is president of her own company, and the other works for a large golf manufacturer.

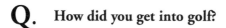

INDUSTRY LEADER Q&A

An interview with Karen Moraghan, President, Hunter Public Relations/Special Events (HPR, Inc.)

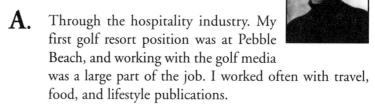

Q. How did you get into golf?

A. Through the hospitality industry. My first golf resort position was at Pebble Beach, and working with the golf media was a large part of the job. I worked often with travel, food, and lifestyle publications.

Q. How would you characterize working at a marketing/ PR agency as opposed to working in a marketing department for a golf company?

A. In an agency, there's a lot of variety. I work as a marketing consultant for the USGA two to three days a week, but I have golf course architects, resorts, golf courses and golf associations as clients. The same skill sets apply as when working for a single company, but with an agency, you learn from previous clients and bring those lessons to the next project.

Q. Do golf-related companies typically want to hire only agencies with golf experience?

A. We try to promote our network of golf industry contacts as a selling point in working with us. Essentially, clients are paying us for our connections. Non-golf agencies have a longer learning curve to understand this industry.

Q. How important is it to know about golf to go into this side of the industry?

A. When we're hiring, we're looking for the right personality to fit in with our office. We want to find people who have basic PR and special events skills and will teach them about golf.

Q. What advice would you give someone who wants to work in marketing for a golf company?

A. Hone your basic skills – writing and communicating, research and use of all electronic media including the Internet. Also, read the golf industry trades. If you want to work with turf equipment companies, read about agronomy.

Q. Networking is such an important part of PR. What associations do you belong to?

A. I'm in the Society of American Travel Writers, the Association of Women in Communications, the National Association of Women Business Owners and the Sunriver Resort Women's Golf Forum in Oregon, which I helped found. This group examines industry issues affecting women golfers, such as identifying the best grass-roots efforts for growing women's golf. I'm also on the National Committee for Special Olympics Golf.

INDUSTRY LEADER Q&A

An interview with Kelly Elbin, Vice President of Communications, Softspikes, Inc., a manufacturer of plastic golf cleats for golf shoes located in Gaithersburg, Md..

Q. How did you get into marketing?

A. Joe Hyman, the president of Softspikes, gave me the opportunity because of my golf background and contacts, and because I communicate and work well with people. He was my mentor.

Q. What was it like to go from being an editor to a golf product marketer?

A. Although I was shifting from editorial to the business end, I was still dealing with many of the same people. It was a fairly smooth transition and the new position allowed me to grow professionally. It was the best thing I could have done at the time because it permitted me the chance to grow within the industry and learn more about how a golf business runs.

Q. **How important is it to know about golf in your field?**

A. Ideally, for sales and marketing, you need to have a real knowledge of the game so that you can speak to the industry. A number of our inside sales reps are former professional players. But even if you're not a golfer, you can learn the industry.

Q. **What advice would you give someone who wants to work in golf marketing?**

A. Learn how the industry works and get to know who the key players are. You can't walk into a golf company and say, "I like golf and want to get into marketing." Employers have too much at risk. They're looking for good communicators who know how the business works. Even working at a driving range for a summer would help give a person some understanding of how the industry operates.

CHAPTER ELEVEN

Careers in the Media

"Despite being a low paying business, there is a certain amount of glamour working as a golf writer. But if you're only looking for that dream-world excitement, it eventually wears off. Hopefully it's replaced by a real love of the job."

George Peper, Editor-in-Chief,
GOLF Magazine

In This Chapter:

- What is the "media?"
- What are the different types of media?
- What does a publisher do?
- What careers are available in television?
- How to find a job as a production assistant
- What about the Internet?
- Learn about the following positions:
    Publisher
    Staff Writer
    Freelance Writer
    Television or Video Producer
    Production Assistant
    Advertising Account Executive
- Interview with George Peper, Editor-in-Chief, *GOLF Magazine*

Our last formal tour stop is near and dear to my heart. It includes careers in writing – like mine – but it takes a broad look at a variety of occupations grouped together under "media."

What do we mean by "media?"

"Media" is an expansive, plural term that covers the different mediums though which information is communicated. "Communication" is the key concept to keep in mind throughout the chapter.

The media includes newspapers, magazines, television, radio, the Internet, and yes, even books like this one. The media are especially important in the golf industry because there are so many levels of communication.

Golf manufacturers communicate with their retailers and suppliers through trade publications. Recreational golfers stay in touch with the industry and improve their games through hundreds of golf publications. Golf courses and retailers communicate with their customers through magazines, newspapers and the Internet. The professional tours communicate with their fans through broadcasts on network and cable television. Everyone in the golf industry, including golfers and golf fans, is affected by the media.

It is no surprise that the media employ many people and offer excellent career opportunities. As the information in this chapter confirms, positions in the media generally do not require expert playing ability, and although formal education is suggested, experience and golf knowledge are most important.

Careers in the media are easier to understand if you divide the media into three categories: print, broadcast (television and radio), and the Internet. Check the National Golf Foundation publications at www.ngf.org for a media directory that lists more than 500 media contacts across all categories.

What positions are available in print media?

There are hundreds of print publications in the U.S. that target golfers. (Actually, there are thousands of publications when club or community newsletters and magazines are included.) Stop by a newsstand and count the many golf magazines. Look for the regional golf magazines at the next resort you visit. Watch your mail for newsletters and magazines from the golf associations you belong to – such as the USGA or your state golf association. Read the sports or golf section of your newspaper. Pick up the in-flight magazine on an airplane – there will be at least one golf article. Check out the sports section at a bookstore. These are all examples of print media in the golf industry.

One of the best ways to understand who works in the print media is to look at the masthead of a magazine. The masthead usually appears on a page following the table of contents and lists the names and titles of those working on the magazine.

One section of the masthead usually identifies the editorial positions – the people who write and edit the copy. Some common editorial titles are: *editor in chief*, *managing editor*, *senior editor*, *associate editor*, and/or *editorial assistant*. In addition, a publication may hire *copy editors* and *fact-checkers*.

The other section of the masthead identifies the *publisher* and the business side of the magazine. It will include titles such as *director of marketing*, *director of advertising*, and *advertising sales associates*.

What does a publisher do?

Every print publication has a publisher. The publisher provides the strategic direction for the business operation of the publication – whether it's an industry newsletter or a newspaper.

In a small publication – perhaps a local golf newspaper, the publisher may wear many hats, selling advertising, and perhaps even editing and writing. In the start-up phase of a publication, the publisher may make the initial financial investment in the publication (such as salaries and printing expenses) while waiting for subscription and advertising revenue to cover the costs.

What are the careers in television?

Many golfers read print publications, but it's probably safe to say that many more watch golf on television. Next time you watch a tournament on TV, wait for the credits to roll at the end of the program and look at all the positions and people who made the broadcast possible.

The most senior position in both television and radio is the *producer*. The producer manages all aspects of a broadcast. Usually a TV producer is an employee of a network or broadcast company. (The PGA TOUR has its own production company, which works closely with the network producers.) There may be several *assistant producers* working for a producer. Working behind the scenes are *directors* and *cameramen*.

There are, however, independent producers who put their own financial resources behind a project and then sell the project to media channels. Special features, such as biographical or historical programs, are generally produced this way.

One entry-level position to the broadcast media is the title of *production assistant*. The job is fairly routine and often involves "logging" video pieces into a database system for later retrieval. If you've wondered how the announcers of a televised tournament can immediately show pre-taped interviews and features, it's because a production assistant organized and logged in these snippets.

To work in golf broadcasting, it is necessary to have a good knowledge of the game and its history. If you are interested in work in television or radio – consider a college that offers a major in broadcasting.

How do I find a position with a production company?

I spoke with Rob Cowen from Cowen Media, Inc., www.cowenmedia.com, a video and TV production company with about 50 percent of its work in the golf industry. Rob spent 10 years with CBS Sports before he and his wife started their company in 1989. Here are Rob's suggestions for getting into production:

- Watch the credits at the end of a televised tournament. Identify the people working in areas that interest you and call them directly. Be prepared to work at routine assignments such as answering the phone or being a "go-for." Experience inside a TV production studio is a powerful résumé builder.
- Look at golf videos in your video store or call The Booklegger (800-262-1556; www.booklegger.com), which is a large golf book/video distributor. Identify video production companies and call them. Independent video producers periodically need interns. The compensation is low (sometimes just gas and lunch expenses), but the experience is excellent. Most entry-level positions (non-internships) in production do not pay more than $25,000 annually.

How do you know you will be good at production? Rob suggests you have three essential qualities: incredible organization, creative problem solving skills and never taking "no" for an answer.

There are also opportunities in television on the non-production side. For example, The Golf Channel sells its programming to local cable carriers and affiliates. ***Marketing coordinators*** employed by The Golf Channel, www.thegolfchannel.com, work with local affiliates in promotions and sales.

What about careers in radio?

If you are interested in careers in radio, a good starting point is PGA TOUR Radio, www.pgatourradio.com, which covers PGA TOUR events and other golf programming. The PGA TOUR Radio Web site lists affiliate stations across the country. Tommy Douglas, the president and CEO of PGA TOUR Radio suggests that if you are just starting, you might want to inquire about internships with your local radio station.

What about Internet careers?

Most of the larger golf Web sites have editors, producers, and marketing and ad sales staffs. The editor charts the editorial content of the site, and hires writers and contributors. Producers handle more technical aspects, like programming and posting stories. (Often, however, the job descriptions for editors and producers overlap.) The marketing and sales staffs promote the site and sell advertising on it.

There are only a handful of financially successful golf Web sites, and often, their budgets are limited. But many offer summer internships for college students. To work at a golf Web site, you must know how the Internet works, and have knowledge of html language, as well as graphics programs like Photoshop and Quark XPress. Passion and knowledge for the game are also essential.

JOB HUNTING TIPS:

Work at a tournament that is televised

Another entry point into production is through working at tournaments (described in Chapter 9) with television coverage and getting to know the production teams. Check the Internet employment sites and search by employer, such as The Golf Channel or PGA TOUR. Also consider positions in non-golf television programming and then use your experience to move into golf productions.

Following are some of the most successful golf Web sites:

➤ www.pgatour.com
➤ www.lpga.com
➤ www.golfonline.com (*GOLF Magazine*)
➤ www.golfdigest.com
➤ www.golf.com

CAREERS TO EXPLORE

Career Close-up: FREELANCE WRITER

OVERVIEW: A *freelance writer* is self-employed and works under contract. This means there is no fixed salary or corporate benefits, such as health insurance. But freelance writers can choose their assignments and often work from home. Many publications – both print and online – prefer hiring freelance writers to save money on salaries and benefits.

DUTIES: Freelance writers may develop their own ideas for articles and suggest them to publications, or, if they are established, they may be contacted by publications offering assignments.

Once a story has been assigned, the writer must conduct required research and interviews, and then write the content. Very often the writer receives a specific word count and deadline from his or her editor.

Although a writer is expected to submit a work in near-final form, the work will be edited, and the freelance writer may be asked to rewrite some parts.

SALARY RANGE: Freelance writers are often paid by the word – $1 per word is common for magazine articles. The average annual salary of an active freelance writer is $45,000, but top producers can earn $100,000 annually. Beginning freelance writers may earn much less – about $25,000 annually.

JOB OPPORTUNITIES: With hundreds of golf publications on the market, the need for skilled writers is substantial. In addition, golf Web sites provide additional opportunities.

Golf magazines; city, state and regional golf publications; golf association publications (such as the USGA's *Golf Journal*), and even airline flight magazines all hire freelance writers.

EDUCATION & TRAINING: A college degree with a major in English or journalism can provide good training, but writing ability and golf knowledge are the most important skills. A job writing about sports for a college newspaper is good training. Writing is a craft, so the more experience and constructive criticism you've had, the easier it becomes.

ENTRY-LEVEL POSITIONS: In order to land a freelance assignment, a writer usually needs to show a portfolio with writing samples, or "clips." Many freelancers began their careers on the staffs of newspapers, magazines or Web sites, which gave them the opportunity to build a portfolio. But freelancers can also begin their careers by impressing editors with their golf knowledge and creative, original story ideas. To get started, you might want to send an editor a "query" – a brief description of a story idea, often with a complete opening paragraph or page. If impressed, the editor may pay for the piece and then assign further stories. When sending queries, is important to be familiar with the missions and needs of the publications you are targeting.

GOLF ABILITY & INTEREST: There are many different topics on which to write – from golf travel to the professional tours – and extensive knowledge of the game is essential for all of them. Most freelance writers aren't great golfers, but they probably play regularly, and know the games' intricacies.

SPECIAL SKILLS & PERSONAL TRAITS: The freelance writer, like any independent contractor, needs strong personal motivation and self-discipline. It also helps to have good people skills, as conducting interviews – sometimes with reluctant subjects – is a big part of the job. Creativity is also important because the most successful freelancers are those with fresh, colorful ideas and writing.

CAREER LADDER & PROMOTION PROSPECTS: The salary potential of a freelancer depends on his or her ability to develop a stable of clients offering steady assignments. A successful writer can write about many different topics in the industry. Some freelancers go on to positions at the publications for which they have worked, or to careers in public relations.

Career Close-up: **EDITORIAL AND STAFF WRITING POSITIONS**

OVERVIEW: *Golf editors and writers* have some of the best jobs in the industry – or at least they think so. Why do they love their jobs so much? Perhaps it's because they have access to some of the best golf courses, and the most interesting people, in the game.

Editors and writers, depending on where they work, often specialize in distinct segments of the game – from travel, to equipment, to golf instruction, to the professional tours. At newspapers, however, golf writers need to be experts in all aspects of the game, as they may be

---

SOUND BITES FROM FREELANCE WRITERS

Positive:

"You make your own schedule."

"There's no commute."

"You play lots of golf."

Negative:

"There's no guaranteed paycheck, health benefits or office camaraderie."

covering their local PGA or LPGA Tour events one week, and then writing about the latest course opening or equipment trend the next week.

DUTIES:

- An *editor in chief* has overall responsibility for the editorial direction of a publication, and is often said to provide the "vision" behind a publication's mission. He or she also is responsible for managerial duties, such as hiring and overseeing staff, and keeping informed on the financial progress of a publication.

- *Associate and senior editors* perform any or all of the following duties: planning editorial content; assigning, editing, researching and writing stories; fact-checking and proofreading. Writers and editors must be informed about nearly all aspects of the industry.

- *Managing editors* coordinate with the printing press, make sure the other editors meet deadlines, and oversee editorial traffic – the process by which stories go from the editors to finished pages in a magazine.

- *Copy editors* and *fact-checkers* make sure editorial content meets style guidelines and is factually and grammatically correct.

- Entry-level positions, such as *editorial assistant* and *assistant editor*, often include many administrative duties, including answering phones and responding to mail. Sometimes they include researching articles for editors and writers and the occasional chance to write.

SALARY RANGE: Beginning editorial assistants and assistant editors earn from $20,000 to $25,000 a year; assistants in the low to high $20s; associate editors from $25,000 to $60,000; and senior editors up to $100,000, depending on seniority and the size of the publication. An editor in chief can make more then $200,000 a year at a large publication. Golf writers at large newspapers are some of the best-paid reporters, often earning from $50,000 to $80,000 a year. Writers at smaller papers make significantly less, and are often asked to cover sports other than golf.

JOB OPPORTUNITIES: It is tough to find people who are expert at journalism *and* extremely knowledgeable about golf, so there are always opportunities for those who meet those criteria.

EDUCATION & TRAINING: A major in journalism is helpful, but not necessary. Writing and editing ability, combined with a love for and extensive knowledge of the game, is most important. In order to be considered for entry-level jobs out of college, a golf writer or editor must have prior experience, so many begin their careers covering sports for their college newspapers and/or interning at golf or sports publications.

ENTRY-LEVEL POSITIONS: Many publications have paid summer internships, which can lead to entry-level jobs as a sports writer at a newspaper, or editorial assistant or assistant editor at a magazine. Entry-level jobs often combine menial work – answering phones, filing and performing tasks for other editors and writers – with the occasional chance to shine as a writer or editor. Once you prove your writing and editing ability, it is not hard to move up.

GOLF ABILITY & INTEREST: Attend a "media day" or press event at a golf course and you will see plenty of goofy golf swings among the participants. While they are generally passionate and knowledgeable about the game, golf writers and editors do not have to be expert players. Most, however, are decent golfers. It helps to know what you are doing on the golf course, because writers and editors are often asked to play in outings, to "rate" new courses, and to interview professional golfers.

SPECIAL SKILLS & PERSONAL TRAITS: Creativity is a must, as editors and writers must present information in clear, new and colorful ways. Editors must also be able to empathize with readers, in order to determine the best ways to reach them. Persistence and organization are key, as writers and editors are often juggling many different projects and trying to track down busy interview subjects. The ability to accept constructive criticism is also crucial; writing (and even editing) is a craft that takes plenty of feedback to hone.

CAREER LADDER & PROMOTION PROSPECTS: The general career path at a magazine is from editorial assistant – an administrative position – to assistant editor, to associate editor, to senior editor, to managing editor, to editor and/or editor in chief. Sometimes, there are deputy editors between the senior and managing editors. As mentioned above, it is difficult to find people who are both talented at editing and knowledgeable about golf, so those who demonstrate skill in both areas are quickly promoted.

The career path in newspapers is from sports writer at a small paper (under 30,000 circulation), to sports writer at a larger newspaper. Only the largest newspapers – and newspapers in areas where golf is popular – have specific positions for golf writers. Those papers include *The New York Times, The Arizona Republic, The Los Angeles Times, The Orlando Sentinel, The Newark Star Ledger* and *The Fort Myers News-Press.*

Career Close-up: ADVERTISING SALES

OVERVIEW: How do golf publications turn a profit? It is not through subscription sales, as many people believe, but through the sale of advertising space. *Advertising account executives* are charged with convincing companies to advertise with *their* publication.

DUTIES: Advertising account executives work much like the sales reps described in Chapter 6 – Careers With Manufacturers. Commissions often account for a large part of their salaries, and they must work hard to cultivate a client base. Clients can come from endemic companies (those in the golf industry, such as club manufacturers) and non-endemic companies (car manufacturers and credit card companies, for example). Sales reps spend much of their time meeting with and entertaining clients and their advertising agencies.

JOB OPPORTUNITIES: There aren't many advertising account executives devoted exclusively to golf – perhaps about 100 combined at the major golf magazines, and dozens more at regional publications, so opportunities are limited.

EDUCATION & TRAINING: A bachelor's degree in business is helpful, and an MBA is increasingly important for top executive positions.

ENTRY-LEVEL OPPORTUNITIES: Advertising account executives typically follow one of two career paths. Most start in entry-level positions at advertising agencies, which plan and place advertising campaigns for companies. A good place to start is the position of *media planner*. A media planner with a few golf accounts will become familiar with both the advertising and golf industries, and should be able to leverage his or her experience and contacts to an account executive position.

Another route is to work as an advertising account executive in the non-golf media – at trade or consumer magazines and newspapers. If you have golf knowledge and the ability to develop a strong, reliable client base, your skills will translate to golf.

GOLF ABILITY & INTEREST: Advertising account executives have to know the game: Many non-endemic advertisers expect their account executive to be a liaison with the golf industry, and endemic advertisers expect account executives to know how the industry works. Account executives also frequently entertain clients on the course; they don't have to be single-digit handicaps, but they must know etiquette and the USGA Rules of Golf.

SPECIAL SKILLS & PERSONAL TRAITS: As with the reps in Chapter 6 – Careers with Manufacturers advertising account executives need to be personable and persuasive. It also helps to have a thick skin; dealing with rejection is a big part of the job.

CAREER LADDER & PROMOTION PROSPECTS: A typical career path goes from working your way up at an advertising agency or non-golf publication, to a position as account executive at a golf publication. The next step is promotion to regional sales manager, then to ad director, and then to associate publisher or publisher.

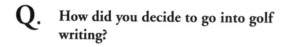

INDUSTRY LEADER Q&A

An interview with George Peper, Editor-in-Chief, GOLF Magazine.

Q. **How did you decide to go into golf writing?**

A. When I left college, I thought, OK, you like writing, you love golf; how do you combine the two? I wrote to the editors of *GOLF Magazine* and *Golf Digest*, but it took some persistence until I got a job.

Q. **What do you look for in job candidates?**

A. When I look at a résumé, I go directly to that bottom line – interests and hobbies. If the first word isn't golf, they aren't going to get hired. Even if golf isn't their favorite hobby, if they aren't clever enough to put it first, then they aren't smart enough to work here!

Q. **How do you decide to which departments your editors are assigned?**

A. Inevitably they tend to gravitate toward one department or another. There aren't too many trained instruction writers, so we'll hire or promote writers with other experience for instruction positions, and then give them the requisite instruction books to study. Some editors have started in instruction and gone on to features. It really depends on their interests and skills.

Q. Do the magazine's writers also provide content for your Web site?

A. We have a staff of 15 at Golfonline.com, and we also encourage the *GOLF Magazine* writers to submit pieces.

Q. Would you steer would-be golf writers to trade publications?

A. That's probably the best way to break in. It's a catch-22 because you need clips – previously published work – to catch an editor's eye. If you're really ambitious, you'll submit articles for free. You can do a story walking along the ropes at a tournament. If it's well-written, and you submit it to your local paper, they may publish it and you may get noticed.

Q. What would you tell would-be writers who have an idealized picture of the job?

A. Despite being a low paying business, there is a certain amount of glamour. But if you're only looking for that dream-world excitement, know that it eventually wears off. Hopefully it's replaced by a real love of the job. My first assignment was the '76 Heritage Classic, and I can still remember the chair I sat in and the questions I asked. I can tell you that even after 25 years, my job has never gotten old – I still love it.

Q. What would you tell someone who wants to work in the golf industry, but isn't sure what area is right for them?

A. In trying to choose any career, try to think back on an episode in your life when you really felt good about yourself. Maybe you had a lemonade stand. Think about why the experience was satisfying and then ask yourself, what talents did you bring to the lemonade stand? Did you paint the sign to attract customers, or did you decide the pricing? Once you know your strengths and interests, seek out the job that will capitalize on those talents.

CHAPTER TWELVE

Other Careers

In This Chapter:

- Careers off the beaten path
- Careers for retirees
- International opportunities
- Learn about the following positions:
    Caddie
    Golf car maintenance
    Golf photographer
    Golf industry lawyer
    Player agent
    Golf coach
    "Emerging" careers

If you have a career in mind and wondered why it has not made the pages of this book so far, keep reading. This chapter includes careers that didn't fit neatly into one of the previous chapters or did not quite meet the five criteria for careers included in the book. The careers are "off the beaten path," or, as a golfer might say "in the rough."

You may recall from the first chapter that there were five criteria for the careers listed in this book. Here they are again:

1. There must be a significant number of positions available.
2. The positions must be those for which training or education is available.
3. The industry sector must be stable or growing.
4. A knowledge of golf must be helpful to the career.
5. Careers should cover a broad range of skills and interests.

Why work as a caddie?

Imagine walking three or more miles on a golf course while carrying a 20-pound golf bag from each shoulder. Unless you are caddying for excellent golfers, your walk will not be in a straight line, and it may take more than four hours. Except at a handful of exclusive courses, caddies seldom make more than $50 per bag for an 18-hole "loop." Why be a *caddie*?

One reason is that you like to play golf – many courses allow caddies to play the course at off-peak times. Another reason is that everything you learn about golf and golfers will make you a more knowledgeable candidate for other jobs in the industry. You may even decide you want to become a full-time professional caddie.

The best way to find a job as a caddie is to visit the ***caddie master*** at a club that offers a caddie program (usually a private club). A local municipal course should be able to provide you with the names of private clubs in your area. A good caddie master will make sure you know some essentials about the game and then will send you out with a more experienced caddie so that you can learn about the course. Many caddies are independent contractors and are not employees of the facility, which means they are not eligible for employee benefits.

If you are a high school student and a caddie, you may be eligible for a college scholarship from the Evans Scholars Program, www.evansscholarsfoundation.com. This Foundation, established in 1930, has chapters at 14 major universities.

If you are interested in a full-time career as a caddie, contact the Professional Tour Caddy Association at www.caddycentral.org, which has more than 140 professional tour caddies as members.

Caddie Master Enterprises, Inc., located in Pinehurst, N.C., manages golf caddie programs for more than 21 private clubs and resorts in 10 different states. Contact 800-391-WALK. CME employs managers, assistant managers and more than 1,500 caddies in its programs. According to CME, all assistant managers are groomed to become caddie masters. A qualified candidate must be willing to travel, have strong communication and organizational skills, and a love for the game of golf and its long tradition. Assistant caddie manager salaries range from $500 to $600 per week.

What are the opportunities in golf car maintenance?

The number of clubs that offer caddies is declining, but the number of golfers using golf cars is increasing. Generally, the head golf professional is in charge of a facility's fleet of golf cars. The car fees often supplement the golf professional's salary. Many golf cars are leased from golf car manufacturers who hire ***mechanics*** and ***technicians*** to keep them in good repair before they are transported to golf courses.

Usually hidden from golfers' view is a garage where cars are recharged (if electric) or refueled (if gasoline-powered). Regular maintenance is required and most of the major car manufacturers sponsor training seminars for ***golf car technicians***. If you have mechanical ability and have been working in another industry, consider applying your skills in a golf environment.

For more information, contact the following golf car companies:

➢ Club Car: www.clubcar.com

➢ E-Z-GO, a division of Textron Inc.: www.ezgo.textron.com

➤ Yamaha Golf Car Company: www.yahamagolfcar.com

What about careers in golf photography?

Golf photography is all around us, whether in an advertising brochure for a new golf resort, part of a feature story in a golf magazine or as fine art in a gallery. A common theme among *golf photographers* is that they all love the game.

There are only about 20 photographers who specialize in and work full time photographing golf courses. There are many other photographers working part time photographing courses or professional golfers in action.

According to one of these course photographers, Mike Klemme, the job of the photographer is to capture the drama of a course. Photo shoots are often early in the morning or at the end of the day, when the light is more dramatic. See Klemme's Web site at www.golfoto.com.

During the recent boom in golf course construction, restoration and renovation, photographers have been busy helping to show off the new links. New business has stabilized, however, and competition among the top course photographers is keen. Realistically, this is a hard career to break into.

I asked Mike what his advice would be to someone just starting out in this career. His suggestion was to find a specific photo style or type of course and build a business around it. For example, he suggested specializing in courses on golf resorts or great public courses. In case you didn't consider it, course photographers do a lot of traveling.

How will a law degree help me in the golf industry?

Choosing law as your profession can create opportunities to work in the golf industry. Many *lawyers* have golf companies or facilities as their clients, work as the in-house lawyer for a golf association, or become *tournament-player agents*. Law is a demanding profession, however, and it is better to love the law than to select the profession because you love golf.

If you are already a lawyer and want to develop more contacts with golf industry clients, consider writing an article for an industry newsletter or publication on a relevant topic. If you have a specialty in corporate law, for example, you might consider an article about the different types of corporations for a start-up manufacturing company. Other issues of interest to golf companies involve trademarks, service marks and patents – all grouped as "intellectual property." Golf developers and facilities are interested in real estate and zoning law, and club membership documents.

Many large golf manufacturers and associations have a permanent "in-house" legal staff. Generally these positions require three to five years' prior experience with a law firm.

How do I become a Tour player agent?

Have you wondered how the names and logos of famous brands appear on famous golfers' hats, bags, shirts and even umbrellas? Although a golfer could make those arrangements himself or herself, the player usually turns over those duties to an **agent** – also called **player's representative**. In addition to managing endorsements, an agent will advise a client on image (clothing, hair style and even temperament), which events or tours to play, and sometimes, financial investments.

Many sports agents are lawyers because endorsements and legal contracts are an important aspect of their work. You may want to consider a law school that offers a concentration in sports management such as Tulane Law School in New Orleans, www.law.tulane.edu.

Where can I obtain information about college coaching?

College sports are supervised by the National Collegiate Athletic Association, www.ncaa.org. There are about 1,000 **college golf coaches** for men's teams, and about 700 for women's teams – with men coaching women and vice versa.

Generally, golf coaches are expert golfers who played collegiate golf and like coaching serious amateurs. It is not necessary to be a member of The PGA of America or the LPGA Teaching & Club Professional Division to coach. The association for female coaches is the National Golf Coaches Association, www.ngca.com. The male counterpart is the Golf Coaches Association of America, www.collegiategolf.com.

What if I am retired but want to work in the industry?

This is your opportunity to turn your avocation into a vocation. Positions as **golf course rangers** and **starters** are commonly filled by retirees.

If after reading this book, you find a match between your previous work experience and a position in the industry, think about beginning a new career in the industry. Your experience and maturity, plus the flexibility in your schedule, may be just what a new employer is looking for.

Where can I learn about international opportunities in the golf industry?

Golf is a global sport and a global business. Here are some suggestions if you like to travel and would like to work outside the United States.

- Check the large manufacturers mentioned in Chapter 6 for those with foreign sales offices and operations.

- Consider employment with U.S. golf course construction firms discussed in Chapter 3. Many are expanding their business overseas.

- Visit the U.S. industry trade shows where manufacturers from outside the U.S. exhibit:

  ➤ The annual PGA Merchandise Show in Orlando and PGA Fall Expo in Las Vegas attract international attendees and exhibitors. See www.pgaexpo.com.

  ➤ The Golf Course Superintendents Association of America trade show held in February also includes many international manufacturers. See www.gcsaa.org

- If you really like to travel, consider golf industry shows in Australia, Spain and Canada organized by PGA Worldwide Golf Exhibitions, a division of Reed Exhibition Companies, also listed on www.pgaexpo.com.

Are there additional careers and occupations in the golf industry?

Absolutely! Ones we don't even know about. Here are some careers and occupations that were not nearly as visible 10 years ago.

- Until recently, there were few golf experts in the fitness area. But a few people realized that they could specialize in *golf physical fitness*, and now this is a growing occupation. It is unusual to read a golf publication without reading about how improving physical strength and flexibility can improve your game.

- Along with physical fitness comes "mental" fitness. My colleagues in the golf industry see *psychological coaching* emerging as a unique profession making a strong contribution to the mental side of the game.

- Not too long ago, the thought of specializing in planning and guiding golf vacations seemed far-fetched. Now, careers in *golf and travel* are here to stay.

- The golf industry is still exploring how to effectively use the Internet. But imagine using real-time video over the internet to analyze your golf swing with your favorite golf instructor hundreds of miles away. It's happening already, and *software developers* are hard at work on improving the technology.

  I hope these last examples encourage you to use *your* skills and imagination to come up with a career just waiting to be discovered.

Since writing this book, my golf game has slipped. I can barely stay focused on the course.

I reach into my pocket for a tee and think about the company that manufactured it. I pull out a ball, notice the logo, and daydream about marketing and the power of a great brand name.

I pull out my driver and consider how long it took for the research and development folks to create it. Out of the corner of my eye, I see a golf car moving along the next fairway. Is that the superintendent riding up to check on that newly planted section of grass?

I haven't hit the ball yet, but I know thousands of people in thousands of careers are part of every shot I make. If only one of them would step forward and drive my ball a couple hundred yards down the fairway! But no such luck.

The good news is that my drive is long. The bad news is that it ends up on a cart path. I pull out my rule book – silently thanking the USGA – and take my relief. Now it's getting cold. I put on a new sweater and remember that it was made by a new company. I wonder how they're doing. As a slight rain begins to fall, out comes one of those plastic rain covers I received as a gift at a charity tournament. What a great job that tournament director did!

So many people in so many careers have made a difference in my game. But what matters to me is that golf makes a difference in *your* life. Whether you are an expert golfer or just an interested observer, there is a place for you in the golf industry. I hope I have helped you find it.

Golf Industry Businesses
and Golf Associations

PGA-Accredited Professional
Golf Management Programs

Golf Industry Businesses & Golf Associations

Acushnet Company
(Manufacturer of golf balls, clubs, shoes, gloves and accessories under the Titleist, FootJoy, Cobra and Pinnacle brand names)
PO Box 965
Fairhaven, MA 02719-0965
Telephone: (508) 979-2000
Facsimile: (508) 979-3909
Web site: www.titleist.com; www.cobragolf.com; www.footjoy.com; www.pinnaclegolf.com

American Golf Corporation
(American Golf manages more than 320 private, resort and daily fee courses in the U.S., U.K. and Australia)
2951 28th St.
Santa Monica, CA 90405-2961
Telephone: (310) 664-4086
Facsimile: (310) 664-6167
Web site: www.americangolf.com

American Junior Golf Association
(Provides positive life experiences for aspiring junior golfers through competitive golf, while setting high standards)
1980 Sports Club Drive
Braselton, GA 30517
Telephone: (770) 868-4200
Facsimile: (770) 868-4211
Web site: www.ajga.org
Email: ajga@ajga.org

American Society of Golf Course Architects
(The American Society of Golf Course Architects (ASGCA) is a non-profit organization comprised of leading course designers)
221 N Lasalle St., Floor 3500
Chicago, IL 60601-1510
Telephone: (312) 372-7090
Facsimile: (312) 372-6160
Web site: www.asgca.org
Email: asgca@selz.com

American Society of Irrigation Consultants
(Provides a forum wherein irrigation design professionals can meet to exchange information and advance skills and techniques in irrigation design, installation and product application)
954 Risa Road, Unit B
Lafayette, CA 94549-3418
Telephone: (925) 516-1124
Facsimile: (925) 516-1301
Web site: www.asic.org

Ashworth, Inc.
(Golf apparel and shoe manufacturer)
2765 Loker Ave. W
Carlsbad, CA 92008-6601
Telephone: (760) 438-6610
Facsimile: (760) 438-6657
Web site: www.ashworthinc.com

Association of Golf Merchandisers
(A non-profit association of buyers and suppliers, The Association of Golf Merchandisers is the educational voice of the golf merchandising industry)
PO Box 19899
Fountain Hills, AZ 85269-1899
Telephone: (480) 836-8250
Facsimile: (480) 836-8251
Web site: www.agmgolf.org

The Association of Disabled American Golfers
(Nation's leading organization in promoting the inclusion of golfers with disabilities into the game and advising the major associations and individuals of the golf community of important issues.)
PO Box 2647
Littleton, CO 80161-2647
Telephone: 303-922-5228
Web site: www.adag.org

Audubon International
(Environmental education programs and
conservation assistance to enhance wildlife habitat
and conserve natural resources)
46 Rarick Road
Selkirk, NY 12158-2104
Telephone: (518) 767-9051
Facsimile: (518) 767-0069
Web site: www.audubonintl.org
Email: acss@audubonintl.org

Belding Sports
(Custom logoed golf bags, carry bags, headcovers,
shoe bags, etc., team-licensed merchandise, limited
editions)
1621 Emerson Ave.
Oxnard, CA 93033-1846
Telephone: (805) 487-7000
Facsimile: (805) 487-0897
Web site: www.beldingsports.com

The Booklegger
(Distributor of golf books, videos, software, training
aids, cards, calendars, art, games and gifts)
PO Box 2626
Grass Valley, CA 95945-2626
Telephone: (530) 272-1556
Facsimile: (530) 272-2133
Web site: www.booklegger.com
Email: order@booklegger.com

Burton Golf, Inc.
(Golf bag manufacturer)
654 Anchors St. NW
Fort Walton Beach, FL 32548-3861
Telephone: (850) 244-8651
Facsimile: (850) 664-0030
Web site: www.burtongolf.com
Email: contact@burtongolf.com

Caddie Master Enterprises
(Provide golf caddie services to resorts and country
clubs desiring five star customer service)
124 Linden Pines Place
Aberdeen, NC 28315-5626
Telephone: (910) 255-0220
Facsimile: (910) 255-0224

Callaway Golf Company
(Manufacturer of Big Bertha woods and irons,
Odyssey putters, and Callaway Golf Rule 35 golf
balls)
2285 Rutherford Road
Carlsbad, CA 92008-8815
Telephone: (760) 931-1771
Facsimile: (760) 929-8120
Web site: www.callawaygolf.com
Email: customerservice@callawaygolf.com

Club Car, Inc.
(Manufacturer of golf cars and carry all turf
maintenance vehicles)
4125 Washington Road
Evans, GA 30809-3067
Telephone: (706) 863-3000
Facsimile: (706) 863-5808
Web site   www.clubcar.com

Club Managers Association of America
(CMAA advances the club management profession
by fulfilling the educational and related needs of its
members)
1733 King St.
Alexandria, VA 22314-2720
Telephone: (703) 739-9500
Facsimile: (703) 739-0124
Web site: www.cmaa.org
Email: cmaa@cmaa.org

ClubCorp USA, Inc.
(Golf facility development and management)
3030 LBJ Fwy, Suite 700
Dallas, TX 75234-7763
Telephone: (972) 243-6191
Facsimile: (972) 888-7583
Web site: www.clubcorp.com
Email: contactus@clubcorp.com

Cowen Media
(Video and television work for companies involved
with golf)
935 Allwood Road, Floor 2
Clifton, NJ 07012-1988
Telephone: (973) 815-0555
Facsimile: (973) 815-0550
Web site: www.cowenmedia.com
Email: info@cowenmedia.com

Crittenden Golf

(Publisher of golf newsletter, magazines, and daily e-news)
PO Box 919035
San Diego, CA 92191-9035
Telephone:　(858) 503-7575
Facsimile:　(858) 503-7588
Web site:　www.crittendenmagazines.com

Cutter and Buck

(Golf product manufacturer–men's and women's apparel, golf footwear, luggage and ties)
2701 1st Ave., Suite 500
Seattle, WA 98121-1179
Telephone:　(206) 622-4191
Facsimile:　(206) 448-0589
Web site:　www.cutterbuck.com
Email:　info@cutterbuck.com

Deere and Company

(Manufacture turf maintenance equipment)
4401 Bland Road
Raleigh, NC 27609-6240
Telephone:　(919) 431-2337
Facsimile:　(919) 431-2680
Web site:　www.deere.com
Email:　al01858@deere.com

Dunlop Slazenger Group Americas

(Manufacture golf bags, balls, clubs, gloves and hats)
PO Box 3070
Greenville, SC 29602-3070
Telephone:　(864) 241-2200
Facsimile:　(864) 241-2395
Web site:　www.maxfli.com;
www.dunlopsports.com; www.slazenger.com

Dynacraft Golf Products, Inc.

(Clubmakers component company)
PO Box 4550
Newark, OH 43058-4550
Telephone:　(740) 344-1191
Facsimile:　(740) 344-6174
Web site:　www.dynacraftgolf.com
Email:　dynacraft@nextek.net

Edwin Watts Golf Shops, Inc.

(Offers a large selection of pro-line equipment – from clubs and bags to shoes, balls, and apparel)
20 Hill Ave. NW
Fort Walton Beach, FL 32548-3858
Telephone:　(850) 244-2066
Facsimile:　(850) 244-5217
Web site:　www.edwinwatts.com

Evans Scholars Foundation

(Sending caddies to college since 1930)
1 Briar Road
Golf, IL 60029-2000
Telephone:　(847) 724-4600
Web site:　www.wildcats.northwestern.edu/es/

Evergreen Alliance Golf Limited

(Golf facility management)
8650 Freeport Pkwy, Suite 200
Irving, TX 75063-1925
Telephone:　(972) 915-3673
Facsimile:　(972) 915-3677
Web site:　www.eaglgolf.com

Executive Women's Golf Association

(Promoting the growth of women's golf in the U.S. and Canada with a welcoming environment for new and experienced golfers)
300 Avenue of Champions, Suite 140
Palm Beach Gardens, FL 33418-3664
Telephone:　(561) 691-0096
Facsimile:　(561) 691-0012
Web site:　www.ewga.com
Email:　mail@ewga.com

Fazio Golf Course Designers, Inc.

(Golf course design)
17755 SE Federal Hwy.
Jupiter, FL 33469-1749
Telephone:　(561) 746-4539
Facsimile:　(561) 746-7503

The First Tee

(To impact the lives of young people around the world by creating affordable and accessible golf facilities)
425 S. Legacy Trail
World Golf Village
Saint Augustine, FL 32092
Telephone:　(904) 940-4000
Facsimile:　(904) 940-1556
Web site:　www.thefirsttee.com

The Golf Academy of the South

(Associate degree program)
307 Daneswood Way
Casselberry, FL 32707-5809
Telephone:　(480) 905-9288
Facsimile:　(480) 905-8705
Web site:　www.sdgagolf.com
Email:　sdga@sdgagolf.com

Golf Around The World
(Manufacturing and distribution of golf training aids)
1396 N. Killian Dr.
Lake Park, FL 33403-1924
Telephone: (561) 848-8896
Facsimile: (561) 848-0870
Web site: www.golfaroundtheworld.com

The Golf Channel
(National television channel devoted to golf, marketing and advertising)
7580 Commerce Center Drive
Orlando, FL 32819-8947
Telephone: (407) 363-4653
Facsimile: (407) 345-4603
Web site: www.thegolfchannel.com

Golf Course Builders Association of America
(A non-profit trade organization comprised of the world's leading golf course builders and suppliers to the industry)
727 O St.
Lincoln, NE 68508-1323
Telephone: (402) 476-4444
Facsimile: (402) 476-4489
Web site: www.gcbaa.org
Email: gcbaa@aol.com

Golf Course Superintendents Association of America
(GCSAA is the professional association for the men and women who manage and maintain golf facilities worldwide.)
1421 Research Park Drive
Lawrence, KS 66049-3858
Telephone: (785) 841-2240
Facsimile: (785) 832-4488
Web site: www.gcsaa.org
Email: infobox@gcsaa.org

Golf Digest
(Publisher of Golf Digest, Golf World, and Golf World Business)
1120 Avenue of the Americas, Floor 8
New York, NY 10036-6700
Telephone: (212) 789-3000
Facsimile: (212) 789-3003
Web site: www.golfdigest.com

Golf Journal
(Official publication of the USGA)
1 Liberty Corner Road
Far Hills, NJ 07931-0708
Telephone: (908) 234-2300
Facsimile: (908) 781-1112
Web site: www.golfjournal.com
Email: golfjournal@usga.org

GOLF Magazine Properties
(Publish GOLF Magazine, the official publications of the PGA TOUR, Senior PGA TOUR, LPGA, and the U.S. Open)
2 Park Avenue, 10th Floor
New York, NY 10016
Telephone: (212) 779-5000
Facsimile: (212) 481-8085
Web site: www.golfonline.com

Golf Range Association of America
(Trade association for owners, operators and developers of golf driving ranges, learning centers and domes; publish Golf Range Magazine)
211 W 92nd St., Suite 58
New York, NY 10025-7438
Telephone: (203) 544-9504
Facsimile: (203) 544-9506
Web site: www.golfrange.org
Email: rangeassoc@aol.com

Golf Writers Association of America
(Membership association for published golf writers)
10210 Green Tree Road
Houston, TX 77042-1232
Telephone: (713) 782-6664
Web site: www.gwaa.com
Email: mhauser806@aol.com

GolfingCareers.Com
(Career site for finding jobs and career information in the golf industry)
2 Commerce Way
Norwood, MA 02062
Telephone: (781) 255-1818
Facsimile: (781) 255-1212
Web site: www.golfingcareers.com
Email: sales@golfingcareers.com

Golfsmith International
(Leading golf equipment cataloger and retailer, also offer a wide variety of personalized items for tournaments, etc.)
11000 N Ih 35
Austin, TX 78753-3152
Telephone: (512) 837-4810
Facsimile: (512) 837-9347
Web site: www.golfsmith.com
Email: comments@golfsmith.com

Golfsurfin.Com
(Job listing service for the golf industry)
10102 Hidden Place
Miami, FL 33156-3265
Telephone: (305) 663-7153
Facsimile: (305) 663-8174
Web site: www.golfsurfin.com
Email: info@golfsurfin.com

The Golfweek Group
(Publishers of GolfWeek and GolfWeek Superintendents News)
1500 Park Center Drive
Orlando, FL 32835-5705
Telephone: (407) 563-7000
Facsimile: (407) 7076
Web site: www.golfweek.com
Email: email@golfweek.com

Greater Cincinnati Golf Association
(Regional Amateur Golf Association)
PO Box 317825
Cincinnati, OH 45231-7825
Telephone: (513) 522-4444
Facsimile: (513) 521-4242
Web site: www.gcga.org
Email: gcga@usga.org

Hyatt Hotels and Resorts
(Owner and operator of hotels and resorts)
6505 Blue Lagoon Drive, Suite 430
Miami, FL 33126-6012
Telephone: (305) 268-4747
Facsimile: (305) 268-4788
Web site: www.hyatt.com

Hunter Public Relations, Inc.
(A full service marketing public relations agency)
41 Madison Avenue
New York, NY 10010
Telephone: (212) 679-6600
Web site: www.hunterpr.com

International Association of Golf Administrators
(The IAGA serves as a medium for golf administrators to exchange information and techniques relating to the game of golf)
3740 Cahuenga Blvd.
North Hollywood, CA 91604-3502
Telephone: (818) 980-3630
Facsimile: (818) 980-6729
Web site: www.iaga.org
Email: iaga@aol.com

International Network of Golf
(1200 plus members, media based networking association whose mission is to enhance and promote communication in golf)
PO Box 951422
Lake Mary, FL 32795
Telephone: (407) 328-0500
Facsimile: (407) 328-0599
Web site: www.inggolf.com
Email: ingdaddy1@aol.com

Irrigation Association
(A non-profit, North American organization, is to improve the products and practices used to manage water resources, and to help shape the worldwide business environment of the irrigation industry.)
6540 Arlington Blvd.
Falls Church, VA 22042-6638
Telephone: (703) 536-7019
Facsimile: (703) 536-7019
Web site: www.irrigation.org

Izod Club
(Golf apparel for men and women)
3 Park Ave., Floor 24
New York, NY 10016-5902
Telephone: (800) 522-6783
Facsimile: (912) 526-4516
Web site: www.izod.com

KemperSports Management, Inc.
(National golf course management and development company: 20+ years of ownership, management and development experience)
500 Skokie Blvd., Suite 444
Northbrook, IL 60062-2867
Telephone: (847) 291-9666
Facsimile: (847) 291-0271
Web site: www.kempersports.com
Email: info@kempersports.com

Ladies Professional Golf Association

(National golf association)
100 International Golf Drive
Daytona Beach, FL 32124-1082
Telephone: (386) 274-6200
Facsimile: (386) 274-1099
Web site: www.lpga.com
Email: lpga@adelphia.net

Lake City Community College Construction Management Program

(Education, golf course OPS, landscape technology, turf equipment, irrigation and forest management)
RR 19 Box 1030
Lake City, FL 32025-8703
Telephone: (904) 752-1822
Facsimile: (904) 755-1856
Web site: www.lakecity.cc.fl.us
Email: piersolj@mail.lakecity.cc.fl.us

Landmark Golf Company

(Golf and development firm whose business is creating prestigious master planned residential and resort communities and designing, constructing and managing high-quality golf facilities.)
74947 US Highway 111, Suite 200
Indian Wells, CA 92210-7137
Telephone: (760) 776-6688
Facsimile: (760) 776-6686
Web site: www.landmarkgolf.com
Email: information@landmarkgolf.com

Landscapes Unlimited, LLC

(Golf course construction, irrigation, renovation, construction mgmt and ownership with 25 years experience and 300 courses)
1601 Old Cheney Road
Lincoln, NE 68512-1402
Telephone: (402) 423-6653
Facsimile: (402) 423-4487
Web site: www.LandscapesUnlimited.com
Email: lui@landscapesunlimited.com

Marriott Golf

(Marriott Golf provides management services to 27 facilities and supports Marriott brands in golf-related business dealings)
6649 Westwood Blvd., Suite 500
Orlando, FL 32821-6066
Telephone: (407) 206-6249
Facsimile: (407) 206-6042
Web site: www.marriott.com

Meadowbrook Golf Group, Inc.

(Own, lease and manage numerous golf courses in U.S.; clients include military bases, universities and municipalities)
331 S. Florida Ave.., Suite 41
Lakeland, FL 33801
Telephone: (863) 686-2376
Web site: www.meadowbrookgolf.com

Metropolitan Golf Association

(Provides clubs with educational and junior golf programs, handicapping tournaments, insurance and the MET Golfer Magazine)
49 Knollwood Road
Elmsford, NY 10523-2813
Telephone: (914) 347-4653
Facsimile: (914) 347-3437
Web site: www.mgagolf.org
Email: mgagolf@mgagolf.org

Mike Klemme Golfoto, Inc.

(Golf photography)
2116 W. Willow Road
Enid, OK 73703-2403
Telephone: (580) 234-8284 or 800-338-1656
Facsimile: (580) 234-8335
Web site: www.golfoto.com

Minnesota Golf Association

(Upholds and promotes the game of golf and its values for all golfers in Minnesota)
6550 York Ave. S., Suite 211
Edina, MN 55435-2333
Telephone: (952) 612-4643
Facsimile: (952) 927-9642
Web site: www.mngolf.org
Email: info@mngolf.org

Mississippi State University

PO Box 5325
Mississippi State, MS 39762
Telephone: 662-325-2323
Web site: www.msstate.edu

Mizuno USA

(Mizuno manufacturers and distributes high performance golf clubs, bags, gloves, shoes and apparel)
1 Jack Curran Way
Norcross, GA 30071-1532
Telephone: (770) 441-5553
Facsimile: (770) 448-3234
Web site: www.mizunousa.com

The National Association of Golf Tournament Directors
(Enhancing the quality and effectiveness of golf tournaments for business, charity and recreation)
212 S Henry St.
Alexandria, VA 22314-3522
Facsimile: (703) 549-9074
Web site: www.nagtd.com
Email: nagtd@aol.com

National Club Association
(A voice for the club community on legal, legislative and regulatory matters and information resources to address club needs)
1120 20th St., NW, Suite 725
One Lafayette Centre
Washington, DC 20036-3459
Telephone: (202) 822-9822
Facsimile: (202) 822-9808
Web site: www.natlclub.org

National Golf Coaches Association
(Encourages the playing of intercollegiate golf for women in correlation with a general objective of education and in accordance with the highest tradition of intercollegiate) competition)
180 North LaSalle Street, Suite 1822
Chicago, IL 60601
Telephone: (312) 551-0814
Facsimile: (312)551-0815
Web site: www.ngca.com

National Golf Course Owners Association
(An international trade association devoted exclusively to furthering the interests of golf course owners)
1470 Ben Sawyer Blvd., Suite 18
Mount Pleasant, SC 29464-4587
Telephone: (843) 881-9956
Facsimile: (843) 881-9958
Web site: www.ngcoa.org
Email: membership@ngcoa.org

National Golf Foundation
(National golf industry trade association: provides golf business research, information and consulting services)
1150 S US Highway 1, Suite 401
Jupiter, FL 33477-7226
Telephone: (561) 744-6006
Facsimile: (561) 744-6107
Web site: www.ngf.org

National Golf Sales Representatives Association (NGSRA)
(Association for all independent and company golf sales representatives; networking and communication to the golf industry)
PO Box 6134
Scottsdale, AZ 85261-6134
Telephone: (480) 860-6348
Facsimile: (480) 860-6919

National Institute of Golf Management
(Offers opportunity for professional enhancement to a broad spectrum of individuals who desire to elevate their knowledge of management, operations and the challenges of the golf business)
Oglebay-Dept. of Continuing Education
Rt. 88 North
Wheeling, WV 26003
Telephone: (304) 243-4019
Facsimile: (304) 243-4106
Web site: www.ngf.org/nigm

National Minority Golf Foundation
(An advocacy and resource center organization working to increase minority participation in the game and business of golf)
7226 N 16th St., Suite 210
Phoenix, AZ 85020-5255
Telephone: (602) 943-8399
Facsimile: (602) 943-8553
Web site: www.nmgf.org
Email: staff@nmgf.org

National Recreation & Park Association
22377 Belmont Ridge Rd
Ashburn, VA 20148-4501
Telephone: (703) 858-0784
Facsimile: (703) 858-0794
Web site: www.nrpa.org

Nevada Bob's Golf
(Offers a large selection of pro-line equipment – from clubs and bags to shoes, balls, and apparel)
8720 E. Frank Lloyd Wright Blvd
Scottsdale, AZ 85260-1926
Telephone: (480) 483-1800
Facsimile: (480) 991-6793
Web site: www.nevadabobs.com

Nike Golf

(Manufacture golf apparel, bags, balls, gloves and shoes)
1 SW Bowerman Drive
Beaverton, OR 97005-0979
Telephone: (503) 671-6453
Facsimile: (503) 671-6376
Web site: www.nikegolf.com

The PGA of America

(The PGA of America, through its 25,000 members, is dedicated to promoting the game of golf to everyone, everywhere)
100 Avenue of Champions
Palm Beach Gardens, FL 33418-3653
Telephone: (561) 624-8400
Facsimile: (561) 624-8448
Web site: www.pga.com

PGA TOUR

(National golf association, professional tour)
112 PGA TOUR Blvd.
Ponte Vedra Beach, FL 32082-3046
Telephone: (904) 285-3700
Facsimile: (904) 285-2460
Web site: www.pgatour.com

PGA TOUR Tournaments Association

(Improve business of all PGA TOUR co-sponsored tournaments and other member events, professional golf information resource)
13000 Sawgrass Village Cir, Suite 36
Ponte Vedra Beach, FL 32082-5023
Telephone: (904) 285-4222
Facsimile: (904) 273-5726
Web site: www.pgatta.org
Email: pgatourta@aol.com

PING, Inc., a Subsidiary of Karsten Manufacturing

(Manufacture golf bags, clubs, accessories, gifts and awards)
PO Box 82000
Phoenix, AZ 85071-2000
Telephone: (602) 687-5000
Facsimile: (602) 687-4482
Web site: www.pinggolf.com

Professional CLUBMAKERS' Society

(An independent professional association promoting and serving professional clubmakers worldwide)
70 Persimmon Ridge Drive
Louisville, KY 40245-5043
Telephone: (502) 241-2816
Facsimile: (502) 241-2817
Web site: www.proclubmakers.org
Email: pcs@proclubmakers.org

Professional Tour Caddies of America

(A non-profit corporation and has worked to improve conditions for PGA Tour Caddies for the past 18 years)
14567 Aqua Vista Ct
Jacksonville, FL 32224-1801
Telephone: (904) 223-1624
Facsimile: (904) 223-1624
Web site: www.caddycentral.org

Rain Bird Sales, Inc. - Golf Division

(Committed to golf course irrigation, using state of the art technology)
970 W Sierra Madre Ave.
Azusa, CA 91702-1873
Telephone: (626) 812-3600
Facsimile: (626) 812-3608
Web site: www.rainbird.com
Email: webmaster@rainbird.com

Ralph Maltby's GolfWorks

(Distributor of golf club components and machines; tools, books, and supplies used to build and repair golf clubs)
4820 Jacksontown Road
Newark, OH 43056-9377
Telephone: (740) 328-4193
Facsimile: (740) 323-0311
Web site: www.golfworks.com
Email: golfworks@golfworks.com

Reebok International, Ltd.

(Manufacture golf shoes, apparel, gloves, and accessories)
1895 J W Foster Blvd.
Canton, MA 02021-1099
Telephone: (781) 401-5000
Facsimile: (781) 401-4000
Web site: www.reebok.com

Reed Exhibition Company

(Golf industry trade shows)
383 Main Ave.
Norwalk, CT 06851-1543
Telephone: (203) 840-5400
Facsimile: (203) 840-9400
Web site: www.pgaexpo.com
Email: inquiry@pga.reedexpo.com

RMY Management Group, L.L.C.

(Premier event management, meeting planning and tournament operation solutions for corporate and association clients)
180 N Lasalle St., Suite 1822
Chicago, IL 60601-2604
Telephone: (312) 551-0810
Facsimile: (312) 551-0815
Web site: www.rmygroup.com
Email: info@rmygroup.com

RYANGOLF (a Division of Ryan, Inc. Eastern)

(Golf course contractor)
786 S Military Trail
Deerfield Beach, FL 33442-3025
Telephone: (954) 427-5599
Facsimile: (954) 427-6305
Web site: www.ryangolf.com
Email: ryangolf@gate.net

SBC FUTURES Golf Tour

(The SBC FUTURES Golf Tour, the official developmental tour of the LPGA, features 20 plus tournaments across the U.S.)
1300 Eaglebrooke Blvd.
Lakeland, FL 33813-4663
Telephone: (863) 709-9100
Facsimile: (863) 709-9200
Web site: www.futurestour.com
Email: golf@futurestour.com

Senior Golfers Association of America

(Host 3-day senior golf tournaments at resorts throughout the country)
3013 Church St.
Myrtle Beach, SC 29577-5820
Telephone: (843) 448-1569
Facsimile: (843) 448-0433

SOFTSPIKES, Inc.

(Manufactures plastic golf cleats)
806 W Diamond Ave., Suite 200
Gaithersburg, MD 20878-1415
Telephone: (301) 738-7756
Facsimile: (301) 548-7458
Web site: www.softspikes.com

Spalding Sports Worldwide

(Offering such brands as Ben Hogan, Strata, Top-Flite and Etonic)
425 Meadow St.
Chicopee, MA 01013-2201
Telephone: (413) 536-1200
Facsimile: (413) 536-1404
Web site: www.topflite.com

Taylor Woodrow Communities

(Developer of high-end golf course communities)
7120 Beneva Road
Sarasota, FL 34238-2850
Telephone: (941) 554-2000
Facsimile: (941) 925-7023
Web site: www.taylorwoodrowhomes.com

TaylorMade-adidas Golf Company

(Golf equipment and apparel manufacturer)
5545 Fermi Court
Carlsbad, CA 92008-7324
Telephone: (760) 918-6127
Facsimile: (760) 918-3576
Web site: www.taylormadegolf.com

Texas Tech University

PO Box 45005
McClellan Hall
Lubbock, TX 79409-5005
Telephone: (806) 742-1480
Facsimile: (806) 742-0980
Web site: www.ttu.edu

Textron, Inc.

(Comprises E-Z-GO Textron, the golf-car industry leader; Jacobsen Textron, the choice of top turf-care professionals around the world; and Ransomes Textron, a leader in turf-care and utility vehicles)
4550 N Point Pkwy., Suite 400
Alpharetta, GA 30022-2420
Telephone: (770) 360-9600
Facsimile: (770) 360-1467
Web site: www.textron.com

Toll Brothers, Inc.
(Builder of luxury homes and golf course communities)
21630 Ridgetop Circle
Sterling, VA 20166-6564
Telephone: (703) 433-6201
Facsimile: (703) 433-6202
Web site: www.tollbrothers.com
Email: airwin@tollbrothersinc.com

The Toro Company
(Provider of maintenance equipment and irrigation systems to golf courses worldwide)
8111 Lyndale Ave. S
Bloomington, MN 55420-1136
Telephone: (952) 888-8801
Facsimile: (952) 887-8258
Web site: www.toro.com/golf
Email: info@toro.com

Troon Golf, LLC
(Golf course management, development and consulting)
15044 N Scottsdale Road, Suite 300
Scottsdale, AZ 85254-8135
Telephone: (480) 477-0448
Facsimile: (480) 477-0575
Web site: www.troongolf.com
Email: jmunson@troongolf.com

TurfNet Associates, Inc.
(Print and web-based information services for golf course superintendents)
21 Brandywine Road
Skillman, NJ 08558-1603
Telephone: (908) 359-3370
Facsimile: (908) 359-3389
Web site: www.turfnet.com
Email: turfnet@turfnet.com

University of Nebraska – Lincoln
1410 Q Street
Lincoln, NE 68508-1650
Telephone: (402) 472-2023
Web site: www.unl.edu

United States Golf Association
(National governing body for golf in the U.S.A.)
Golf House
Liberty Corner
Far Hills, NJ 07931
Telephone: (908) 234-2300
Facsimile: (908) 234-2178
Web site: www.usga.org
Email: usga@usga.org

United States Golf Teachers Federation
(Worldwide organization that trains and certifies golf teaching professionals)
PO Box 3325
Fort Pierce, FL 34948-3325
Telephone: (561) 464-3272
Facsimile: (561) 461-5636
Web site: www.usgtf.com
Email: info@usgtf.com

USGolfJobs.com, a Divison of (C.M.I.)
(Source for golf industry employment worldwide)
7960 N Hayden Road, Apt A209
Scottsdale, AZ 85258-3229
Telephone: (801) 720-9734
Facsimile: (801) 720-9734
Web site: www.usgolfjobs.com
Email: usgolfjobs@usgolfjobs.com

Wadsworth Golf Construction Company of the Midwest
(Golf course construction company)
1901 N Van Dyke Road
Plainfield, IL 60544-7727
Telephone: (815) 436-8400
Facsimile: (815) 436-8404
Web site: www.wadsworthgolf.com
Email: wgccmw@aol.com

Wilson Sporting Goods Company
(Wilson Golf focuses on developing technologically advanced products that help the average golfer improve their golf game)
8700 W Bryn Mawr Ave., Suite 3
Chicago, IL 60631-3507
Telephone: (773) 714-6600
Facsimile: (773) 714-4570
Web site: www.wilsonsports.com

The Women's Golf Company
(Retailer of women's golf apparel)
PO Box 222
Arlington, VT 05250
Telephone: (800) 984-7324
Web site: www.womensgolf.com

World Golf Foundation
*(Management of the World Golf Hall of Fame, Walk
of Champions, World Golf Village and The First Tee
initiative)*
21 World Golf Place
World Golf Village
Saint Augustine, FL 32092
Telephone: (904) 940-4000
Facsimile: (904) 940-4390
Web site: www.wgv.com

The Wrenfield Group Inc.
*(Develop and manage promotional and cause-
related events for amateur golfers at golf and
country clubs nationally)*
PO Box 579
Ridgefield, CT 06877-0579
Telephone: (203) 438-0090
Facsimile: (203) 431-9265
Web site: www.rallyforacure.com
Email: twg@ridgefield-ct.com

Yamaha Golf Car Company
*(Manufactures of golf cars, utility vehicles, and
Yamaha genuine parts and accessories)*
1000 Highway 34 E
Newnan, GA 30265—2132
Telephone: (770) 254-4000
Facsimile: (770) 354-4158
Web site: www.yamahagolfcar.com

PGA-Accredited Professional Golf Management Programs

Arizona State University

Professional Golf Management Program
7001 E. Williams Field Road, #20
Mesa, AZ 85212
Telephone: (480) 727-1017
Facsimile: (480) 727-1186
Web site: www.east.asu.edu/msabr/pgm

Contact: Richard Grinage, Director
Program Established: 1999
Alumni: n/a
Freshman Students 2000/2001: 50 – 45 men, 5 women

Handicap Admission Requirement/GPTP Playing-Ability Test Assistance:
Guide of 8 for men and 10 for women. Offer four levels of player development classes with PGA Professionals.

Degree:
Bachelor of Science in Agribusiness with a concentration in Professional Golf Management from the Morrison School of Agribusiness.

Career Aspirations of Students Upon Graduation:
Head Golf Professional
Director of Golf Operations

Highlights of Program:
Agribusiness; high level of expertise in food and beverage, i.e., food retailing, food safety.

Campbell University

Professional Golf Management Program
PO Box 218
Buies Creek, NC 27506
Telephone: (910) 893-1395; (800) 334-4111, ext. 1395
Facsimile: (910) 893-1392
Web site: www.campbell.edu/business/pgm

Contact: Kenneth Jones, PGM Director
Program Established: 1999
Alumni: n/a
Freshman Class Students 2000/2001: 81 – 79 men, 2 women

Handicap Admission Requirement/GPTP Playing-Ability Test Assistance:
Recommended 8 for men and women. Unlimited use of the university-owned golf courses and practice range. Students can receive unlimited golf instruction and video analysis. Student tournament program consists of at least 15 events each semester.

Degree:
Bachelor of Business Administration from the School of Business

Career Aspirations of Students Upon Graduation:
Director of Golf
General Manager
Head Golf Professional

Highlights of Program:
Each semester a golf class is provided that covers the materials of the Golf Professional Training Program (GPTP). Students who qualify academically are eligible to enter the 3/2 program: in five years, students can earn both a BBA and an MBA degree through the School of Business.

Clemson University

Professional Golf Management Program
263 Lehotsky Hall
Clemson, SC 29634
Telephone: (864) 656-3400
Facsimile: (864) 656-2226

Contact: Dr. Dan Drane
Program Established: 2001
Alumni: n/a
Freshman Class Students 2000/2001: First class accepted for 2001/2001

Handicap Admission Requirement/GPTP Playing-Ability Test Assistance:
Absolute requirement of 8 for men and women.

Degree:
Bachelor of Science from the Department of Parks, Recreation and Tourism Management.

Career Aspirations of Students Upon Graduation:
Head Golf Professional

Highlights of Program:
Program will have a specialty in serving golfers with disabilities.

Coastal Carolina University

Professional Golf Management
PO Box 261954
Conway, SC 29528-6054
Telephone: (843) 349-2647
Facsimile: (843) 349-2455
Web site: www.coastal.edu

Contact: Andy E. Hendrick, Director of Professional Golf Management
Program Established: 1999
Alumni: n/a
Freshman Class Students 2000/2001: 75 - 73 men, 2 women

Handicap Admission Requirement/GPTP Playing-Ability Test Assistance:
Absolute requirement of 8 for men and women. Individual instruction is available upon request.

Degree:
Bachelor of Science in Marketing with a PGM designation from the Wall College of Business Administration.

Career Aspirations of Students Upon Graduation:
Head Golf Professional
General Manager
Director of Golf Operations

Highlights of Program:
More than 50 courses allow Professional Golf Management students free access.

Ferris State University

Professional Golf Management Office OR Admissions Office
1506 Knollview Drive
Prakken Bldg, 420 Oak Street
Big Rapids, MI 49307
Telephone: (231) 591-2380
Facsimile: (231) 591-2839
Web site: www.ferris.edu/htmls/colleges/business/pgm

Contact: Matt Pinter, Professional Golf Management Program
Program Established: 1975
Alumni: 1,183
Freshman Class Students 2000/2001: 80 – 75 men, 5 women

Handicap Admission Requirement/GPTP Playing-Ability Test Assistance:

Handicap of 8 for both men and women is an absolute requirement for admission. Special classes in GPTP courses and numerous teaching seminars, as well as an intensive playing schedule for PGM students are offered to help them pass the GPTP playing-ability test.

Degree:

Bachelor of Science in Business with a major in Marketing/PGM Option from the College of Business Marketing.

Career Aspirations of Students Upon Graduation:

PGA Professional
Other Golf-related Industries

Highlights of Program:

The first Professional Golf Management program in the country. Hundreds of alumni working all over the world; excellent networking capability. More than 1,400 internship sites.

Florida State University

Dedman School of Hospitality
1 Champions Way
University Center, Building B, Suite 4100
Tallahassee, FL 32306-2541
Telephone: (850) 644-4787
Facsimile: (850) 644-5565
Web site: www.cob.fsu.edu/ha/pgm

Contact: Jim Riscigno, Director Professional Golf Management
Program Established: 1999
Alumni: n/a
Freshman Class Students 2000/2001: 26 - 25 men, 1 woman

Handicap Admission Requirement/GPTP Playing-Ability Test Assistance:
Must pass PAT within first year with a maximum handicap of 8 for both men and women. Dr. Ernie Lanford, Internship Coordinator, has been a collegiate golf coach for 20 years as well as a PGA Professional. Ernie works with students to help them improve playing skills and pass the PAT.

Degree:
Bachelor of Science from the College of Business with a major in Hospitality from the Dedman School of Hospitality and a concentration in Professional Golf Management. The PGA of America provides graduates with certification as a Class A PGA Professional.

Career Aspirations of Students Upon Graduation:
Tour Player
Golf Professional at a club or resort
Teaching Golf Professional
Pro-Manager
Director of Golf
Golf Industry Management in corporate, retail, equipment, or manufacturing

Highlights of Program:
With the combination of business degree, hospitality major and PGA certification, students will be drawn toward the management side of the business. This program is unique, with a hospitality major that requires substantial studies in food service, lodging, private club management, golf management, agronomy, hospitality accounting and cost controls, strategic management, and managing service organizations. The College of Business is an AACSB accredited business college and ranked in the top 34 undergraduate programs in the country. The Hospitality major is ranked in the top five nationally by industry and gives students the necessary tools to handle all aspects of the golf industry.

Methodist College
5400 Ramsey Street
Fayetteville, NC 28311
Telephone: (910) 630-7144
Facsimile: (910) 630-7254
Web site: www.methodist.edu

Contact: Jerry Hogge, Director
Program Established: 1986
Alumni: 320
Freshman Class Students 2000/2001: 86 - 76 men, 10 women

Handicap Admission Requirement/GPTP Playing-Ability Test Assistance:
Absolute requirement for men 8; for women 12. Weekly tournaments are held to help students pass the GPTP playing ability test.

Degree:
Bachelor of Science/Bachelor of Arts in Business Administration with a concentration in Professional Golf Management from the Reeves School of Business.

Career Aspirations of Students Upon Graduation:
PGA Professional

Highlights of Program:
PGA certified. On-campus golf course for students only.

Mississippi State University

Professional Golf Management Program
P.O. Box 6217
Mississippi State, MS 39762
Telephone: (662) 325-3161
Facsimile: (662) 325-1779
Web site: www.msstate.edu/dept/pgm

Contact: Scott Maynard, Director
Program Established: 1985
Alumni: 362 in 32 states and 2 foreign countries
Freshman Class Students 2000/2001: 58 - 54 men and 4 women

Handicap Admission Requirement/GPTP Playing-Ability Test Assistance:
All students must have a certified USGA handicap of 8 or less. This is an absolute requirement. All students are required to pass the PGA Playing Ability Test prior to graduation. Two Class A PGA Golf Professionals are on staff and outside teaching professionals conduct seminars each semester.

Degree:
Bachelor of Business Administration in Marketing with a concentration in Professional Golf Management from the College of Business and Industry, Marketing Department.

Career Aspirations of Students Upon Graduation:
Class A PGA Golf Professional
Teaching Professional

Highlights of Program:
Program is limited to 200 students, with 40 to 60 admitted each year. The 18-hole championship golf course was constructed for the PGM program and was voted one of the top-ten university courses east of the Mississippi River by *USA Today* in 1999. Students have unlimited access to this facility. Students co-op one Spring/Summer combination and one Summer/Fall combination. These two eight-month work blocks allow a student to see transitions into and out of the golf season. Other programs at MSU dedicated to the golf industry include a Golf and Sports Turf Management

Program, a Landscape Architecture Program with a concentration in golf course design, and a Landscape Contracting Program for golf course construction.

New Mexico State University

Professional Golf Management Program
Box 30001/Dept. PGM
University Avenue/Business Complex #207
Las Cruces, NM 88003
Telephone: (505) 646-2814
Facsimile: (505) 646-1467
Web site: http://cbae.nmsu.edu

Contact: Pat Gavin, Director
Program Established: 1987
Alumni: Approximately 300
Freshman Class Students 2000/2001: 40 – 32 men, 8 women

Handicap Admission Requirement/GPTP Playing-Ability Test Assistance:
Men: 4; Women: 8. Work with all students on both GPTP and PAT. Students have access to the golf course every day of the year. Offer required PGM classes as well as seminars to help with GPTP.

Degree:
Bachelor of Business Administration with a major in Marketing from the College of Business/Department of Marketing.

Career Aspirations of Students Upon Graduation:
PGA Head Professional

Highlights of Program:
The weather is probably the best of any school. Requirements of handicap plus grade point average of 3.0 or higher attracts the best-qualified individuals. Have a tournament program that is second to none, with yearly payouts of approximately $90,000.

North Carolina State University

College of Natural Resources
Campus Box 8004
NC State University
Raleigh, NC 27695
Telephone: (919) 515-8792
Facsimile: (919) 515-3276
Web site: http://natural-resources.ncsu.edu/pgm

Contact: Dr. Michael Kanters, Director
Program Established: 2002
Alumni: n/a
Freshman Class Students 2000/2001: n/a (first-year class estimated between 30 and 40)

Handicap Admission Requirement/GPTP Playing-Ability Test Assistance:

Handicap of 8 for both men and women is used as a guide for admission. Opportunities for significant play and practice at NC State and area golf courses, PGA Professional mentor program, and golf skills tracking program combine to provide assistance to students.

Degree:

B.S. Professional Golf Management from the Department of Parks, Recreation & Tourism Management.

Career Aspirations of Students Upon Graduation:

Head Golf Professional

Highlights of Program:

Environmental stewardship and leisure services administration. NCSU also has a strong turf management program that will develop a specific turfgrass course for the Professional Golf Management students.

Penn State University

Professional Golf Management Program
201 Mateer Building
University Park, PA 16802
Telephone: (814) 865-7034
Facsimile: (814) 863-8992
Web site: www.hrrm.psu.edu/pgm/homepage.htm

Contact: Stevie Lovell, Assistant Director
Program Established: 1991
Alumni: 120
Freshman Students 2000/2001: 55 – 54 men, 1 woman

Handicap Admission Requirement/GPTP Playing-Ability Test:

Absolute requirement of 8 handicap for men and women. For assistance in passing the GPTP, golf instruction is provided by the Professional staff at the

Penn State Golf Course; teaching and swing seminars are taught by PGA Master Teaching Professionals.

Degree:
Bachelor of Science in Recreation and Park Management with Professional Golf Management option from the School of Hotel, Restaurant and Recreation Management.

Career Aspirations of Students Upon Graduation:
Head Golf Professional
Director of Golf
General Manager
Marketing or Sales in the golf industry

Highlights of Program:
Outstanding academic reputation of Penn State. Strongly business-based curriculum pulls courses from four main departments: Recreation and Park Management, Business, Hotel and Restaurant Management, and Turfgrass Management. Both the Recreation and Park Management and the Hotel and Restaurant Management programs are in the top-five schools nationally in their respective fields. Turfgrass Management is the number one school in its field, and the Smeal College of Business is top rated for public universities and in the Big 10.

INDEX OF PROFESSIONS

F

Fact-checker 116, 121
Financial Analyst 28
Financial Director 16
Financial Officer 58
Food and Beverage Director 45
Food and Beverage Manager 40
Foreman 51
Freelance Writer 119

G

General Manager 30, 40, 42
Golf and Travel 131
Golf Car Technician 128
Golf Course Designer 28
Golf Course Developer 27
Golf Course Ranger 130
Golf Course Superintendent 50, 52
Golf Editor and Writer 120
Golf Instructor 2, 80, 89
Golf Photographer 129
Golf Physical Fitness 131
Golf Professional 80, 87
Golf Teacher 80
Golf-enthusiast Developer 29

H

Head Golf Professional 71, 87
Horticulturist 50
Hotel F&B Manager, Assistant
    Manager 46
Human Resources Director 16

I

Independent Sales Rep 2, 60, 64
Inside Rep 60
Irrigation Consultant 30
Irrigation Designer 30, 35
Irrigation Installation 35
Irrigation Management 35
Irrigation Specialist 50, 54
Irrigation Superintendent 35
Irrigation Technician 51, 54

J

Job or Project Superintendent,
    Construction 34

L

Lawyer 129
Legal Director 16

M

Management Companies 29
Manager 50
Managing Editor 116, 121
Manufacturer's Rep 60
Marketing 58, 106
Marketing and Sales 105
Marketing Assistant 109
Marketing Coordinator 118
Marketing Director 20
Mechanic 50, 128
Media Coordinator 111
Media Director 16
Media Planner 123
Media Relations 96
Meeting Planner 99
Membership Director 16, 20
Merchandise Buyer 70, 71, 74
Municipal Developer 29

N

Natural Resource Manager 37
Not-for-profit Developer 29

O

Operations Manager 96

P

Player's Representative 130
President, Association 15
President or CEO, Manufacturer 66
Pro Shop Assistant 43
Producer 117
Product Designer 58
Product Development and Design 65
Product Manager 58
Production Assistant 117
Professional Associations 16
Project Director, Association 16
Project Manager, Association 19
Project Manager, Facility
    Development 30, 33
Psychological Coaching 131
Public Relations Consultant 106
Publications Director 20, 109

ABOUT THE NATIONAL GOLF FOUNDATION

The National Golf Foundation is a leading research company that provides information and insights on the business of golf. Founded in 1936, the NGF now has more than 6,000 members representing a broad cross-section of the industry including golf equipment manufacturers, golf and consumer media, golf facilities and golf ranges; golf course architects, builders and developers; golf retailers, golf associations and turf maintenance suppliers. The NGF's extensive library offers publications on everything from developing and operating golf facilities to golfer demographics and consumer spending.

NANCY BERKLEY

Nancy Berkley is a noted golf writer and consultant. She writes for the National Golf Foundation, the industry leader in golf research and business information. In addition, she is a contributing editor for *Golf For Women* magazine and the women's feature columnist for *The Golf Insider*, a golf and travel newsletter.

Nancy is the author of *Women's Golf Programs That Work – Best Practices and Case Studies; For Golf Facilities, Teachers, Organizations and Event Planners*, published in 1999 by the National Golf Foundation. This book is required reading for the LPGA professional certification program. She also is the author of several articles including *Handicap How-to's*, (Golf For Women, April 2000) and *Invest 36 Hours and Play in Your Corporate Golf Outing*, (Working Woman, 1999).

In 1998, after a career as a lawyer and marketing executive, Nancy founded Berkley Consulting, Inc. and The Woman's Only Guide® to Golf to share her long-time passion for golf and help grow the game. She speaks and consults on a broad range of strategic initiatives for golf facilities, associations and manufacturers.

Nancy participated in the 20/20 Golf Summit, a conference of golf industry leaders, held at The World Golf Village in November 2000. She was on the Planning Committee of the LPGA 50th Anniversary celebration in October 2000. In addition, she is a member of the Sunriver Resort Women's Golf Forum, which regularly convenes women leaders from the golf industry to address issues of common interest.

An accomplished corporate executive, Nancy held a number of senior positions with Prudential Insurance Company of America including assistant general counsel, vice president, Strategic Planning, and vice president, Corporate Marketing & Business Integration. Prior to joining Prudential, Nancy was an attorney with Sullivan & Cromwell, a Wall Street law firm. Nancy began her professional career as a high school teacher.

Nancy holds a bachelor's degree in political science from the University of Minnesota; a master's degree in teaching from Harvard University Graduate School of Education and a law degree from Rutgers University School of Law, where she was a member of the Law Review. She is a graduate of the Program for Management Development at Harvard Business School.